UnChristian America

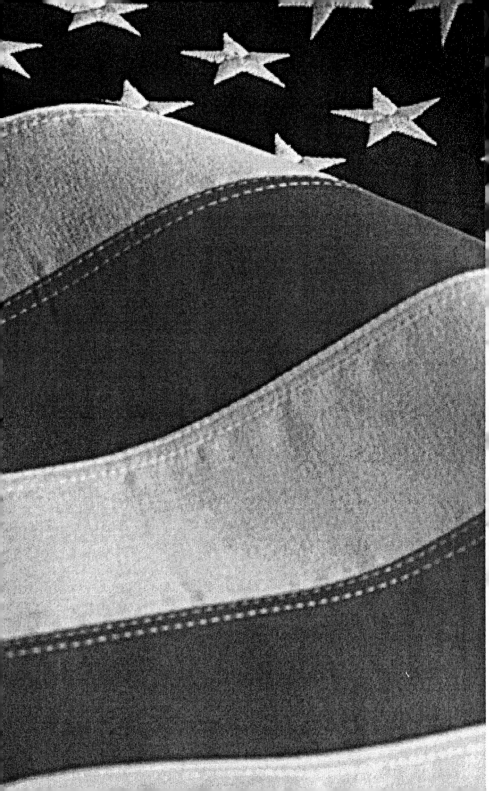

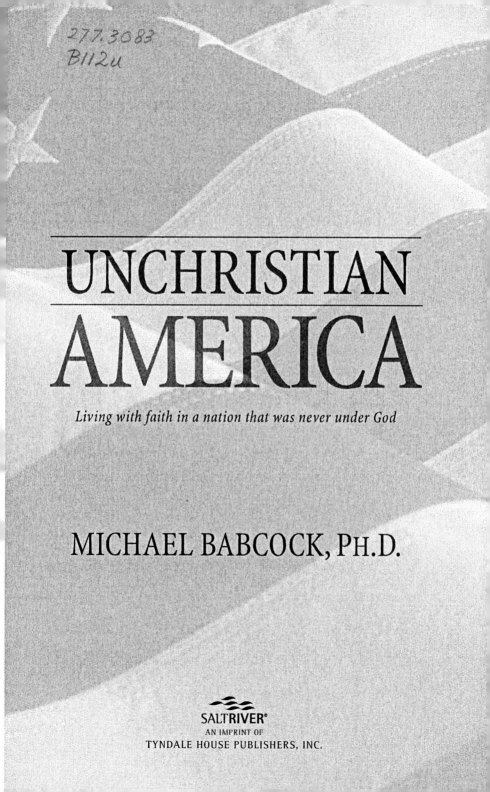

UNCHRISTIAN
AMERICA

Living with faith in a nation that was never under God

MICHAEL BABCOCK, Ph.D.

SALTRIVER®
AN IMPRINT OF
TYNDALE HOUSE PUBLISHERS, INC.

Visit Tyndale's exciting Web site at www.tyndale.com

TYNDALE is a registered trademark of Tyndale House Publishers, Inc.

SaltRiver and the SaltRiver logo are registered trademarks of Tyndale House Publishers, Inc.

UnChristian American: Living with Faith in a Nation That Was Never under God

Designed by Ron Kaufmann

Library of Congress Cataloging-in-Publication Data

Babcock, Michael A.
    Unchristian America : living with faith in a nation that was never under God / Michael A. Babcock.
        p. cm
    Includes bibliographical references.
    ISBN-13: 978-1-4143-1860-8 (sc)
    ISBN-10: 1-4143-1860-X (sc)
    1. Evangelicalism—United States. 2. Christianity and culture—United States. I. Title.
    BR1642.U5B33 2008
    277.3'083--dc22   2008009982

Printed in _____

14 13 12 11 10 09 08
 7   6   5   4   3   2   1

☆ ☆ ☆

[dedication to come]

☆ ☆ ☆

CONTENTS

INTRODUCTION

The dead face stared back at me as I knew it would. I couldn't help taking a peek. I was a thirteen-year-old boy, after all, and it was an easy thing to turn around in the cab of the Toyota and peer down at the body wrapped up like a rug in the back of the truck.

It was night in Central Africa, and night in Africa is always dark. I turned back around to see the dirt road ahead of us and the occasional flash of animal eyes disappearing into the bush.

"Just wait until we get to the village," Bob told me. "You'll never see anything like it again. Funerals really bring out the heathen in them."

Bob was my dorm father at the boarding school. He was a seasoned missionary, but his comment puzzled me, since this man—this dead man we were transporting back to the village of his birth—had been a pastor.

I braced myself for what I could only imagine would be a chilling scene. What would death in an African village look like? I conjured up scenes of women wailing as they beat their breasts and threw themselves on the ground. I could already hear the hypnotic pounding of drums and see the eerie flickering of the fires.

I turned around to look one more time into the frozen, leathery face of a man in his forties. Why, I wondered, was Bob preparing me for what we'd see in the village? This man had been a Christian who worshiped

Jesus. He had turned his back on the gods of his ancestors, gods of stones and sticks.

"We're here," Bob said as the dirt road turned into a clearing of thatched-roof huts. There was a large fire burning, just as I'd expected. But as we came to a stop and got out of the truck, I heard singing. The villagers were singing hymns—in the rhythms and chanted intonations of tribal music. But they were Christian hymns nonetheless. Here in the "heart of darkness" (as Joseph Conrad called it) was the light of the gospel. This light, I came to learn, shines no matter how dark the culture may be. This light, the "light of the glorious gospel," as Paul called it (2 Corinthians 4:4, kjv), still shines brightly after two thousand years because it's not the product or exclusive monopoly of any culture, including my own.

This would become a benchmark experience for me, one I'd think back on years later when struggling over how to be a Christian in an increasingly secularized America. In particular, I remember that night in Africa whenever I hear someone say that Christianity is on the decline. As the millennium approached, American theologian and Jesus Seminar publicist Burton Mack declared, "It's over. We've had enough apocalypses. We've had enough martyrs. Christianity has had a two thousand–year run, and it's over."[1] But Burton Mack never heard hymns in an African village. He didn't know Mananga, the old pastor with white hair. When Mananga smiled, which was often, you could see the incisors that had been sharpened to a point many decades before when he was a young man in a tribe of cannibals. The American missionaries I grew up among may have been tone deaf to the nuances of cross-cultural dialogue, but they earnestly believed that the gospel can change lives, families, even entire villages, for the better.

The great error that scholars like Burton Mack make is to tie Christianity to the institutions, culture, and history of the Western world.

Certainly, it would come as a great surprise to those in the villages of Africa, Asia, and Latin America that "it's over" for the church. We can learn much from the non-Western church about living with faith in the midst of an unbelieving world.

Christianity is not a product of the Western world, the way Burton Mack arrogantly assumes. Cloistered in the ivory towers of theology departments, scholars like Mack fail to recognize the vibrancy of Christian faith in Kenya or India or Guatemala. Nor do they see the vitality of evangelical faith in neighborhood churches all across America. All they see are the dead skeletal remains of a bankrupt social gospel. Mack doesn't speak for Christianity, and he's certainly not authorized to write its obituary. But what makes Mack interesting is how he embodies a certain type of secularism that has overtaken the West—and is gradually overtaking America as well. Mack thinks he's dancing on the grave of Christianity, but it's only a cultural Christianity, not the real thing.

We've lost the cultural battle. We've lost the "Christian" America we thought we had but never really did. Everywhere we see the forces of secularism advancing against the revealed truths of God. But this should not alarm us. Christ is triumphant. The spiritual war has been won at the Cross. That's the message I learned many years ago as the fires flickered in an African village. Along the way, I forgot the message, I lost touch with its power, and I had to learn it all over again.

And that's the story of this book.

☆

My family and I returned to the States during the bicentennial year of 1976. It was a confusing place for a missionary kid who had become a teenager in Africa and suddenly found himself in a world of disco, Jaws, and Happy Days. Other things confused me too, including the strange new mix of politics and religion. Time magazine declared 1976 "the Year of the Evangelical," and the phrase "born again" entered the mainstream vocabulary of our culture. When Jimmy Carter ran for president as a peanut farmer who taught Sunday school, millions of Christians embraced him with hope. America seemed ready for renewal after the long nightmare of Vietnam and Watergate, and evangelical Christians were beginning to explore what role they might play in making it happen.

This was the political world I came of age in—a world in which Bible-believing Christians like myself were determined to "make a difference," to stem the tide of moral decay in our nation and return it to its Christian roots. These were my values, and this became my vision of what Christianity could be expected to achieve in the world. The visceral understanding of the gospel that I gained in Africa—that the gospel is the power of God unto salvation—was becoming a distant memory.

Looking back, the moral and political trends that were under way in American life now seem inescapable. The cultural battle lines that were established during these turbulent years would shape the next generation. "Red states" and "blue states" had not yet been designated—that would have to wait until the divisive presidential elections of 2000 and 2004—but a great cultural divide was already forming in America. In 1973 abortion had become a constitutionally recognized right. In Dade County, Florida, Anita Bryant led a successful campaign to overturn a local ordinance that outlawed discrimination against homosexuals. Across the nation, the drive to ratify the Equal Rights Amendment (the ERA) was met with fierce and growing opposition as critics began to contemplate—and sensationalize—the dark possibilities. Would men and women be forced to share unisex bathrooms?

These issues were like political nitroglycerin in their combination of moral and religious values, cultural expectations of social norms (such as "traditional" gender roles), and the raw struggle for political power. The rise of the Religious Right—arguably the most significant development in American politics at the close of the last century—would be rooted in these struggles. Some victories would be won, such as the defeat of the ERA, though this success would prove to be moot. The American family has been breaking down for the past generation, and we don't have the ERA to blame. As for abortion, this "right" is now so well entrenched within our political culture that the most evangelicals can expect from their political leaders is a sympathetic press release every January 22 "regretting" the moral tragedy of abortion. The gay rights movement in the 1970s was so small and ineffective that Anita Bryant, a former beauty queen who sold orange juice on TV, was able to defeat it. Not so today. Now among the most powerful and well financed of all lobbying blocs, the "homosexual community" (as it is called) will settle for nothing less than an official state endorsement of same-sex marriage.

Who lost America?

The last decades of the twentieth century witnessed the steady dissolution of the traditional two-parent American family. MTV took over the role of guiding America's youth toward adulthood. The personal computer and the Internet transformed our way of life, but some of the earliest homesteaders in this new frontier were pornography kingpins who discovered rich sources of revenue and millions of new addicts. On college campuses, cultural relativism was packaged as "political correctness" and spread like a virus into every corner of American society. Intellectuals, like alchemists in reverse, transformed truth into a base political category—something we construct and negotiate for personal gain. Whether or not Americans could recognize the names of Jacques Derrida or Roland Barthes, they were becoming positively French in their skepticism of truth and meaning. No one seemed immune to this new spirit of relativism, not even the president of the United States, who struggled under oath to define the meaning of the third-person singular present indicative form of the verb "to be." All this occurred against the backdrop of fervent and sophisticated political activism by the Christian Right.

Who lost America?

For over thirty years, evangelical Christians have been waging a vigorous counteroffensive against the forces of secular humanism in American culture. Pastors have been mobilized to "wake up" their congregations and "take back America." Millions of new voters have been registered, and millions of dollars have been spent. Scores of candidates have been endorsed: many good ones, but some really bad ones too—people you'd never dream of inviting home for dinner. Christian conservatives have invested time, money, and reputation in the fortunes of the Republican party. And what do we have to show for it? The movement that burst onto the political landscape in 1980 with such hope and promise has not aged gracefully. Leaders have been forced to step down in disgrace. Religious conservatives are steadily losing clout at the polls as moral issues are trumped by economic and national security concerns. Some Christian lobbying groups have suffered splits over policy disputes. If evangelical Christians at the height of their political power could not take back America, then how is a weakened movement likely to succeed in the years to come?

A generation later, a fierce culture war still rages on many fronts— over the meaning of life, the nature of truth, the definition of a family. These are the main battlefields, the Antietam and Bull Run of this new civil war, but it's the raids and skirmishes that attract most of the attention. Should intelligent design be taught alongside evolutionary theory in our classrooms? Can Christian organizations be compelled to employ someone who is openly gay? Are decency standards no longer enforceable in an age of digital communication? Are Christmas trees religious symbols, and if so, should they be replaced with "holiday trees"? The issues are great and small, serious and often trivial, but every battle in this culture war seems to come back in the end to the question of our national identity—whether we are, bone and marrow, a Christian nation that has lost its way, or whether the "faith of our fathers" is irrelevant to the public policy debates in the new millennium.

How do we relate our faith to our culture? This was the question that Tertullian, the third-century church father, often returned to in his writings. When he famously asked, "What has Athens to do with Jerusalem?" Tertullian was referring to the intellectual values of the Hellenistic world—the philosophical legacy of ancient Greece and Rome. But he also had something to say about the street culture of Rome, the nationalistic myths of the Empire. Since there wasn't a word that captured what he wanted to say about "the qualities of being Roman," Tertullian made one up: Romanitas—the Roman equivalent of Americanism. Until the emergence of Christianity, the Latin language had no need for a word like Romanitas to describe the social, political, and moral values of the Roman Empire. Never a very self-reflective people, the Romans had defined themselves by their actions in the world; they saw themselves as a people of destiny, specially chosen by the gods to "rule mankind and make the world obey."[2] Christianity challenged Rome's most basic set of values. This peculiar, mysterious religion had forced a distinction—a grand clarification—between what it meant to be a Roman and what it meant to be a Christian. The early church fathers were quite aware that they were Roman citizens, but they also understood that their faith in Christ transcended the political and social values of their world.

As American evangelicals, we are far too comfortable with the idea that we, like the ancient Romans, are a special people uniquely called to do God's work in the world. We forget that Jesus turned to fishermen, not politicians, when He began His ministry; we forget that He empowered the twelve disciples with the Holy Spirit, not political charisma, to build His church. No nation, no matter how good and how strong, has ever superseded the mandate that Christ Himself entrusted to His followers. Tertullian understood an important truth that evangelicals need to reclaim: Christians of every age and every culture must "audit" their beliefs in light of Scripture. Audit literally means "to hear"—and that's exactly what we must do. As a community of believers, we must hear the Word of God, not the voices of the world. We must be willing to place our most cherished cultural values alongside Scripture to see what matches up and what falls short.

Who lost America? In the following pages I'll present an answer we don't like to hear: America was never ours to lose.

Some claim that America began its moral decline in 1962 when the Supreme Court "took God out of the classroom." Others would point to the rebellious drug culture of the 1960s, the rise of feminism, or the gay rights movement. But the battle for America wasn't lost that recently. It was lost several hundred years ago at the dawn of the modern world. Yes, America has been a beacon of hope and freedom in the world. Yes, America is great because America is good, as Tocqueville wrote nearly two hundred years ago. Yes, our Founding Fathers invoked God's name in nearly everything they wrote. But America has also been a four hundred–year laboratory experiment in living out the humanistic values of the modern age. As we move deeper into the new millennium, the pace of secularization is accelerating. How Christians respond to the emerging post-Christian America will be determined not just by our theology but by our view of history as well. Christians who are committed to turning back the tide of secularism in America fail to realize that our country, like the rest of the Western world, has been trending post-Christian right from the start.

☆

The first part of this book, "Losing the Battle," examines the intellectual machinery that drives our political activity as evangelicals. I'll argue
that the real enemy we face has never been godless Communism, the gay
lobby, the abortion industry, or the Hollywood elite. The real enemy is
the same one Jesus confronted two thousand years ago: the materialistic
values of this world system. For us today, this worldview is expressed in
a godless secularism that would reduce all of human experience to the
collision of atoms in a purposeless universe. We see the spirit of the age
in the public mockery of our faith and the purging of Christian imagery
from public life. But we didn't arrive at this point overnight; what we're
witnessing in American culture today is the culmination of a battle that's
been raging for several hundred years.

Evangelicals who have entered the political process, however, have
done so in response to more immediate cultural factors. Chapter 1, "The
Battle Is Engaged," presents a historical sketch of the rise and fall of the
Religious Right over the past generation, from its triumphant entry onto
the political stage in 1980 to the collapse of Ralph Reed's 2006 campaign in
Georgia. This is not a comprehensive history—there are many good ones
that have been written—but a personal interpretation of the compromises
that doomed the movement from the start. The central miscalculation of
the Religious Right has been its failure to recognize the real nature of the
battle, how long it's been waged, and the high price we've been willing to
pay for entry into the political theater. I write as an evangelical Christian
who once believed that America is a Christian nation that lost its way. I'm
still an evangelical Christian, but I no longer believe that this nation, or any
nation in this fallen world, can be truly "under God."

The next three chapters tackle the false assumptions that lie beneath our political activism. If, for example, we believe we're a Christian nation that has lost its way, then we'll be striving to "take back America" for God. Chapter 2 argues that while history and culture give us a contradictory picture of our religious heritage, Scripture speaks very clearly to this point. No nation has a special calling from God to do His bidding in the world. Chapter 3, "Rethinking the Shining City," addresses another set of false assumptions—ones deeply embedded in our cultural DNA. The belief that America is an earthly utopia, a nation of practical, self-reliant, and devout men and women, will be placed alongside Scripture and once again found wanting. Evangelicals have also wrongly assumed that the moral and spiritual decline of America has begun in our own lifetime. Chapter 4, "The Long Defeat," will connect our history to the much longer narrative of the Western world. We'll see that Christianity has been under assault since the birth of the modern age five hundred years ago. In the end, I'll conclude that the cultural battle for America is all but lost. We are becoming the post-Christian nation we were always destined to be.

But there's a positive message here as well. The second part of the book, "Winning the War," refocuses our attention on the spiritual victory that Christ has won at the cross. In chapter 5, "Back to the Beginning," I'll present the case that we must look beyond our culture, beyond our history, to the work that God has always been doing in creation, in individual hearts, and in the life of the church. Once we come back to basics, back to the opening chapters of Genesis, we can pose the question that drives chapter 6: "What's Worth Fighting For?" The answer is found, once again, in the beginning—in the core value of life. Before the nations were founded, before human laws were framed, our Creator inscribed this divine attribute into the structure of creation. Life is the prime value of the Christian faith. We were created in the image of God to be vessels for His glory, and we cannot be silent about the sanctity of life. The materialistic worldview denies the character of our Creator. When we speak up in defense of life, we are ultimately bearing witness to the goodness and sovereignty of God.

But it's not enough to hold a biblical position on life. We must demonstrate a biblical approach to living. We must do a better job of modeling the abundant life we have in Christ before an unbelieving world. In the end, I conclude that a biblical view of culture can liberate us from the impossible task of attempting what God never commissioned us to do. The final chapter, "A Simple Call to Virtue," brings us back to our scriptural mandate to live virtuous and godly lives in this present age. To be "peculiar" people who testify to the transforming power of God's grace. To live lives empowered by His Spirit, not by the fleshly tools of this world system.

☆

From the catacombs of ancient Rome to the edge cities of modern America, living for Christ has always meant the same thing: commitment and self-sacrifice, dying to self and dying to the world. By absorbing the values of the larger culture, evangelicals have neglected their responsibility—a responsibility placed on every successive generation of believers—to present a relentless critique of our fallen world:

> That ye may be blameless and harmless, the sons of God, without rebuke, in the midst of a crooked and perverse nation, among whom ye shine as lights in the world. **PHILIPPIANS 2:15 (KJV)**

Instead, the American church has accumulated the cultural baggage of four centuries. As evangelicals, we have tethered our faith to social, political, and economic institutions. Our task should be to critique these relationships and strip our faith of the comfortable, extrabiblical debris of culture—even if this means tossing out some of our most cherished heirlooms.

An audit is long overdue. I, for one, am weary of the world's noise, the incessant din of commerce, the shouting matches of political competition. I'm longing for the church to hear the quiet voice of God, not the blaring trumpets of political victory. I'm longing to hear again the sound of voices singing in a distant village.

PART 1

LOSING
THE
BATTLE

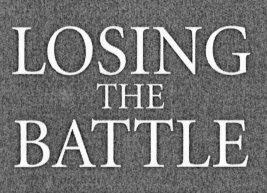

CHAPTER ONE

The Battle Is Engaged

*With the founding of the Moral Majority in 1979, evangelicals and
fundamentalists ventured into the political process. They were not welcomed
with open arms by either the political or religious establishments. Rather,
they kicked down the door and marched in with such fury that they sent panic
through most sectors of American society.*

—CAL THOMAS AND ED DOBSON

I grew up in central Washington, in that wonderful valley ringed by
snowcapped mountains and adorned with apple trees, near places with
Indian names like Wenatchee and Wapato and Walla Walla. Summers
were filled with vacation Bible schools, Kool-Aid ice pops, and warm
evenings with little balsa planes that cost ten cents each at the neighborhood store. Our little white church sat on a street corner and held about
a hundred souls on a good Sunday morning. It was a conservative flock,
and our pastor was a faithful custodian of the law. Dancing was wrong.
Movies were wrong. Long hair for boys was wrong. The Beatles were
wrong. Mixed bathing—I didn't even know what this was, but I knew it
was *wrong*.

Granted, my memories have acquired the softened edges of a
Norman Rockwell painting over the years. But peel away the sentiment,
the nostalgia, the church potlucks, and the flannel graph Bible lessons,
and you see the dark stirrings of cultural fear. America was changing in

the age of the Cold War, the Vietnam War, the Civil Rights Movement, and the British Invasion. The sense of peril was most evident in the first political book I remember, *None Dare Call It Treason*, a high-pitched screed that came out in the middle of Barry Goldwater's disastrous run for the White House in 1964. One of the heroes of the book was still a hero in our quarters—Senator Joe McCarthy, the man who ruined lives with his reckless accusations. Some of our church deacons were even "John Birchers," the kind of people who believed that fluoridation was a Communist plot to take over America through our water supply. It seemed to make sense at the time.

This was the old conservative movement, shaped in the teeth of the Cold War. In this dark geopolitical landscape, America was cast as a Christian nation facing godless Communism. Morality was an indicator of our national strength, our ability to face down the Communist threat. Moral weakness—as evinced by long hair, rhythmic music, and psychedelic drugs—would lead to military weakness. All you had to do was connect the dots. After all, didn't Rome fall when Rome became immoral? As a child I never questioned the history behind that claim. I didn't know that Rome, having been Christianized, was actually *more* moral when it fell than when it ruled the Mediterranean world. But when you're battling spiritual and cultural decline, even bad history can be a good sermon illustration.

Politics was politics in the old conservative movement, and church was church. Those boundaries were seldom crossed, except to denounce moral decay. Those of us sitting in the pews might have shared a common demographic profile, but we didn't talk about it in church. For all his legalism, our pastor taught the Bible faithfully—and drily. His weekly exposition, along with the steady stream of missionaries that came through our little church, would transform my family. Before long my parents felt God calling them to the mission field. This was the way you changed the world back then, long before the church discovered politics. So off they went to Bible school and then to Europe for language training. Finally, in the early 1970s, the Babcock family ended up in the Central African Republic, which was about as far from central Washington as you could get. I look back now and see Africa as the great divide in my life.

The sights and sounds and smells of Africa would be forever etched into my childhood memories. I loved hearing the village drums at night and the warm equatorial rain as it pounded down on the aluminum roof. The open market was colorful and smelly with fresh fruits and vegetables, the *pili-pili* peppers so common across Africa, gunnysacks of flour and sugar, and Arab women who smeared their bodies with goat milk. When we came to buy meat, the Sudanese cowherd would slaughter a bull on the spot and load the carcass, flies swarming and blood running, onto the back of our pickup truck. But it was the evangelistic trips deep into the bush that I remember most. My parents, my brother, and I would gather a crowd with our instruments—three trumpets and an accordion. I was on the accordion. Dad presented a simple Bible lesson, usually a story with flannel-graph illustrations, and gave the gospel message around the interruptions of village goats, pigs, and chickens.

It was in Africa, as a child, that I first read the Bible. There was no television or video games, but that's not why I read. I had a hunger for the Word of God. I first read through the Bible from cover to cover as a twelve-year-old. And then I read it again. I memorized Galatians. I was presumptuous enough to begin writing a commentary on Colossians. The cadences and odd vocabulary of the King James Bible became familiar to me as a child (which made reading Shakespeare a whole lot easier later on). The Bible had transformed my parents' lives, and it would do the same for mine. Not immediately, though. I was a young legalist-in-training, "zealous for the law," as Paul described himself. But I was also hiding God's Word in my heart—and God's Word would not return void. These were the contradictions in my life. On the one hand, I was idealistic and earnest, striving after God with a sense of mission and purpose. But it was all law with no grace. It was my effort, and the only thing my effort yielded was dead religiosity. Years later I would recognize the same contradiction in the political fortunes of the Religious Right. I would also come to see that this contradiction—the tug-of-war between this kingdom and the next—was central to the American character as well.

RUMBLINGS OF DISCONTENT

We returned in 1976 to a very different America. The Vietnam War was over. Watergate had come and gone. My family settled not on the West Coast but in the tobacco fields of South Carolina, in an old plantation town called Hartsville. It was a town with two public schools, one black and one white. I attended neither. Instead, I attended a private Baptist school that had been founded, like scores of others across the Deep South, during the decade of desegregation. I had left Africa behind only to find myself in an all-white school operated by an all-white church.

As a teenager suddenly reintroduced into American culture, I was becoming acquainted with a second strain of American conservatism, one rooted in the Old South and its social and religious conservatism. The Barry Goldwater movement I was familiar with had viewed moral decay as part of the global struggle against Communism. This new movement, in its best form, championed small government and family values; in its worst form, it viewed moral decay through the dirty screen of racial politics. These two cultures would come together in a movement set to explode on the political scene in 1980 with the election of Ronald Reagan and the rise of the Religious Right.

I was a living contradiction. A Westerner in the Deep South.

The descendant of a Union abolitionist family in the heart of the old Confederacy. A young man whose friends in Africa had been black children, now attending an all-white school in a still largely segregated town. A young man who had seen the power of the gospel in the heart of darkness, being drawn toward the empty political promises of a shining city on a hill.

During high school I became interested in politics. The first issue that really captured my attention was the Panama Canal Treaty in 1978. I remember writing a letter to Senator Ernest Hollings and objecting *in the strongest terms possible* to this surrender of American property—this symbol of our ingenuity and sacrifice. But it was a security issue too, since we couldn't let this vital national resource fall into Communist hands. *And so on and so on.* I wrote the letter on wide-ruled paper so there'd be plenty of room for cosignatories. Then I canvassed my fellow high school students and sent the letter off to Washington. I received a warmly patronizing response from the senator's office, and when I listened to the vote on the radio I was disappointed to hear the white-haired senator with his deep Southern drawl say, "Aye" on final passage of the treaty.

Three decades later it's clear to me that Senator Hollings was right and I was wrong.

But I was on board with the movement—the new conservative movement that jumbled up politics and religion and nationalistic pride and jingoism. I was too young perhaps to see the contradictions in any of this. I was balanced awkwardly between worlds—between Africa and America, between childhood and adulthood, between the past and the present, between two views of my country. I was at that time in life when you're trying hard to catch your balance and hold it long enough to figure out where you're standing. Perhaps I was too young to understand that we come to God with all our contradictions, all our paradoxes, all our contrary impulses, and we find completeness in Christ. Certainly I was too young to realize that God didn't have a policy position on the Panama Canal Treaty.

All through the late 1970s this new movement would begin to coalesce around a few distinct themes—moral, cultural, political, and economic. The moral theme was motivated principally by *Roe v. Wade*, the Supreme Court decision in 1973 that established the right to abortion as the "law of the land." As long as abortion was a matter for individual states to take up, as long as it was only whispered about, shuffled off to the rhetorical back alleys of American politics, then Christians weren't terribly concerned about it. But no longer. Abortion was now front and center in American life. More than any other issue, the fight to overturn *Roe v. Wade* unified religious conservatives across the theological spectrum, giving them a sense of purpose and validating those first uncertain steps into politics. But this didn't happen immediately. Perhaps it took some time for the full significance of the Supreme Court's decision to register among conservatives, but that lag time (a period of several years) has opened the door for some critics to question how big a factor abortion really was in the birth of the movement.

Abortion was just one element of a "perfect storm" gathering in the mid- to late-1970s. When the commissioners in Dade County, Florida, passed an ordinance in 1977 outlawing discrimination against homosexuals, Anita Bryant—a former beauty queen and spokeswoman for the Florida Citrus Commission ("A day without orange juice is like a day without sunshine")—stepped forward to "lead a crusade to stop it as this country has not seen before." A prolonged media circus, more like a cultural *Gong Show*, had been set in motion. Rallies were held. Gay activists organized an orange juice boycott. The former beauty queen even took a cream pie in the face at a rally in Des Moines, Iowa. A few months later the ordinance was repealed, and Bryant took her campaign nationwide. Momentum was on her side.

The battle was won without working up a sweat. But the war was just beginning. Religious conservatives weren't the only ones organizing and entering the political arena. The "homosexual community" came out of the closet as a demographic unit with considerable capital and political clout. Long associated with San Francisco and Greenwich Village, homosexuals would become a mainstream part of American culture within a generation. In the early 1980s, the AIDS epidemic provided the newly minted Gay Rights Movement with the cultural mandate it needed to change its public image once and for all.

Meanwhile, the boycott of Florida oranges was successful. Anita Bryant's contract was not renewed in 1979. In 1980 her marriage broke up and her career was in decline. The evangelical community that had held her up as an icon of family values now abandoned her. But the movement she'd helped to launch found new leaders—and new battles.

Moral issues merged inevitably into cultural ones. In the mid- to late-1970s it looked as though the twenty-four words in section 1 of the Equal Rights Amendment were destined to become part of the U.S. Constitution. But that was before another conservative "Joan of Arc," a constitutional lawyer named Phyllis Schlafly, skillfully mobilized conservative opposition around the defense of traditional values. The feminist movement had come of age in America, but by taking on the U.S. Constitution, its leaders had tackled too much—too fast. The amendment expired in 1979, having fallen three states short of the thirty-eight needed for ratification. Though the language of the amendment itself was fairly innocuous ("Equality of rights under the law shall not be denied or abridged by the United States or by any State on account of sex"), Schlafly perceived that a larger game plan had been set in motion. The social fabric of American life could be reshaped, Schlafly warned, by a legion of activist lawyers with the full backing of the Constitution. But this is not why the ERA failed. A cultural nerve had been struck. The role of women was changing in American society—sometimes for the better and sometimes for the worse. Ironically, many of the changes most feared by conservatives have happened anyway, such as widespread acceptance of women's roles in the military. These changes have happened in spite of the ERA's defeat, which should cause us to question how effective our political activity really has been.

New political themes were also emerging—sometimes in strange ways—and these themes would become staples of conservative rhetoric. For example, Hal Lindsey's popularization of biblical prophecy, *The Late Great Planet Earth* (1970), can be read from the distance of almost forty years as the blueprint for a crude evangelical foreign policy. From a conservative standpoint, everything wrong with international affairs was embodied in the cold, academic figure of Henry Kissinger, national security adviser and secretary of state in the 1970s. Lindsey's apocalyptic best seller sketched out the direction evangelicals would take when thinking (for the first time) about foreign affairs in the years following Kissinger's "shuttle diplomacy" in the Middle East, the détente with the Soviet Union, and the opening of diplomatic contacts with China.

Before Hal Lindsey, there was no cohesive evangelical foreign policy. The revival of interest in end times prophecy, however, provoked questions about the larger world and how our actions as a nation might fit into God's plan. In one slim package—a little book with corny chapter titles like "Russia Is a Gog" and "Sheik to Sheik"—evangelicals would find a foreign policy that addressed the major hot spots in the world: the Middle East, the Soviet Union, the European Common Market, and China. The centrality of Israel in biblical prophecy guaranteed its centrality in evangelical foreign policy. Evangelical leaders were unabashedly pro-Israel and soon earned for themselves the label of "Christian Zionists." The role of Gog and Magog in the prophecies of Armageddon ensured that Russia (then the Soviet Union) would be vigorously opposed. Détente would be rejected in favor of a more robust posture toward Soviet expansionism. Christian conservatives, for example, were deeply skeptical of the Strategic Arms Limitation Treaty (SALT II) and opposed it vigorously. The European Common Market was viewed suspiciously too, as it was widely understood by evangelicals to be the forerunner of the revived Roman Empire prophesied by Daniel. Military and political support of Taiwan (another policy position taken by evangelical leaders) found its rationale in China's role in biblical prophecy. Never a favorite of conservatives, China was the nation that would bring two hundred thousand troops against Israel in the battle of Armageddon.

The Late Great Planet Earth became the best-selling nonfiction book of the 1970s. Millions of readers, including the future president of the United States Ronald Reagan, devoured the breezily written and thinly documented book. Of course, Reagan didn't get his foreign policy from Hal Lindsey, but the fact that Lindsey's apocalyptic vision was so compatible with Reagan's political philosophy goes a long way toward explaining why Reagan and the Religious Right embraced each other with such affection.

These apocalyptic themes resonated with the political realities America faced in the world at the time. The nation was longing for a resurgence of American power. After Vietnam and Watergate, we felt like a nation in decline. The picture of a U.S. marine helicopter lifting off from the embassy roof in Saigon in 1975 became an iconic representation of our national disgrace. Two weeks later the Khmer Rouge seized a U.S. container ship, the SS Mayaguez, in international waters off the Cambodian coast. The ensuing mission to rescue the crew only managed to deepen the embarrassment. The Americans had already been removed for questioning, so the marines ended up seizing an empty ship. Most of the crew members were subsequently found floating safely on a Thai fishing vessel; three more were never located. But the impression was once again reinforced that America was a shrinking giant in the world.

When the nation turned to an inexperienced Southern governor in 1976, the general feeling was that Jimmy Carter couldn't do any worse. Four years later, the general feeling was that somehow he had. Carter wanted to bring moral purpose to American foreign policy, but his emphasis on human rights only conveyed a sense of collective guilt. Conservatives were outraged at the "blame America" subtext of all this lecturing on human rights. And when Carter "gave away" the Panama Canal in 1978, conservatives believed that America was presenting the face of weakness to the world. Before long, Communist insurgencies were on the march in Central America, the Soviet Union rolled its tanks into Afghanistan, and fifty-two Americans were held hostage in the U.S. embassy in Tehran.

Nothing captured the sense of political decline more than the Iran hostage crisis. During the final year of the Carter administration, the world watched a helpless America wring its hands. I was a first-semester college freshman at the time, and I remember watching Ted Koppel report on the diplomatic crisis on the show that would later become *Nightline*. Every night the somber music cued up as the title appeared on screen: "America Held Hostage" (as the show was initially called). And every night the show bluntly reminded us how many days America had been held hostage. Day 168, Day 223, Day 345—all the way through the 1980 election. Ronald Reagan couldn't have purchased a more effective TV commercial for his campaign.

My own political values were shaped by these dramatic events. I was a serious student who actually paid attention to what was going on in the world. Disco and *Stars Wars* hadn't made a dent on my imagination. But geopolitics certainly did. Where I had been a child who voraciously read the Bible, compulsively outlined passages, and memorized entire Epistles, I was now a young adult who pored over the voting records of U.S. senators and followed international events with an intensity I once reserved for Matthew Henry's commentary.

Meanwhile, my legalism, which had been nurtured in the doctrinaire culture of a fundamentalist church in the Deep South, took a bitter turn. Our youth pastor suddenly packed up and moved away without even saying good-bye. Nothing was said about it in church, but everybody soon heard through the rumor mill about his multiple affairs and his relationship with a teenage girl in the church youth group. It would be a few years before I would fully recognize the body blow that cultural Christianity had delivered to my spiritual life. I wasn't able to put my finger on what was happening in my life, but I knew I was tired of my own legalism and hypocrisy—and I didn't know what to replace them with. Though I remained sympathetic to the "conservative cause," I was walking away—step by step—from my childhood faith. I had always expected to study the Bible and go to the mission field. But by the time I entered college in 1979, political science seemed the logical choice of study for me. I directed my intellectual passions toward the study of this world, disregarding in the process the great trade-off I was making. My passion for the things of God was dying.

The election of 1980 was approaching, and it was an exciting time to be a political science major. Now there was a new player on the national political scene, one that I was still culturally and politically sympathetic with—the Religious Right. And this movement gravitated naturally toward Ronald Reagan, who spoke our language fluently. To these moral, cultural, and political messages that had been developing for a decade, Reagan added an economic message of low taxes, small government, and free trade. He closed the deal with the nation—and secured the undying loyalty of the Religious Right.

A MOVEMENT IS BORN

As early as 1976, conservative activist Richard Viguerie had predicted that "the next major area of growth for conservative ideology and philosophy is among the evangelicals." Viguerie was among the core activists—along with Paul Weyrich and Howard Phillips—who recognized that the conditions were right for religious conservatives to enter the political fray. They had found a natural ally in Ronald Reagan, and all that was now lacking was the catalyst to move them into politics.

Paul Weyrich, one of the movement's original architects, tells of the unlikely series of events that kick-started the Religious Right as an organized movement. According to Weyrich, it ultimately took the Internal Revenue Service to pull evangelicals into the political ring. That happened in 1978. Evangelical Christians had voted in large numbers for the "born-again" farmer from Georgia, but they were quickly disappointed with his policies on social issues and foreign affairs. Disappointment turned to outright hostility, however, when the IRS issued new guidelines that would have removed tax-exempt status from thousands of fundamentalist schools, largely across the South. The kind of all-white school I was attending suddenly found itself in the crosshairs of the tax collector.

Specifically, the IRS ruled that private schools would lose their tax-exempt status if they had been established during the time of court-ordered desegregation and if the number of minority students currently in the school was less than one-fifth the percentage of minority children in the local community. It wasn't widely known at the time, but these guidelines weren't drawn up originally by the Carter administration at all. Jimmy Carter, whose presidency was one long example of bad timing, was implementing a policy formulated several years earlier. The IRS had trained its sights on "discriminatory" private schools as early as 1970. President Nixon was well aware of the policy and endorsed it on July 10, 1970, in a statement issued by the White House:

> The President approves of and concurs in the IRS decision regarding tax exemption for discriminatory private schools. He believes that ultimately the tax status of racially discriminatory private schools will be determined by the courts and that this is desirable.

Nixon went on to affirm "at the same time" his belief that private schools offered "diversity" and "strength" to the American educational system and that a continuation of their tax-exempt status was desirable for those implementing a "racially nondiscriminatory admissions policy."

The perception that these schools practiced active discrimination was wrong, but there can be little doubt that many of them were in fact started as a direct response to court-ordered desegregation. This was the unspoken history we all understood at schools like the one I attended in South Carolina. Desegregation was the hot political issue when private schools began to pop up across the South. In 1961, nine black students in Rock Hill, South Carolina, sat down at a whites-only lunch counter in a downtown store and refused to leave. In 1962 a young black man named Harvey Gantt won a long legal battle to be admitted to Clemson University. In 1963 the private Baptist school that I would later attend opened its doors for the first time. By the strict letter of the IRS guidelines, my school would have lost its tax-exempt status. It was established in the throes of desegregation, and the percentage of minority students was considerably less than the arbitrary threshold set by the IRS. When I attended in the late 1970s, the school's minority population stood at 0 percent.

Of course, there's another story told about the founding of these schools, a more favorable narrative that emphasizes moral outrage at "God being taken out of the classroom" with the 1962 Supreme Court decision on school prayer. There can be no doubt that *Engel v. Vitale* reverberated throughout America. Billy Graham described this as "another step toward the secularization of America." Senator Sam Ervin of North Carolina declared that "the Supreme Court has made God unconstitutional." This event fixed itself in the collective memory of religious conservatives because it seemed to clarify the whole picture of what was going wrong with America in the 1960s. Student uprisings, the drug culture, the sexual revolution—all of this could be explained as the logical consequence of taking God out of the classroom.

In the years following the 1962 decision, school prayer figured prominently in the grand narrative of loss and restoration that conservative Christians began telling about their nation. Forget that the practice was never universal. Forget that the prayers were mostly ceremonial recitations performed in unison. Forget that Christian children have always had the right to pray to their heavenly Father whenever, wherever, and however they desire in the solitude of their own hearts. What mattered was the symbolism of it all. What mattered was that this one court decision came to represent the loss of a Christian America.

School prayer became the "backstory" that explained the existence of these schools after the fact. Who could blame Christian parents if they wanted to shelter their children from the godless trends of public education? But throughout the South in the 1960s and 1970s, God was no more—and no less—a presence in public schools than He had ever been. The one conspicuous change within the larger culture, though, was the desegregation of public schools. Among the students I went to school with, some were there because their parents (mine included) wanted a traditional Christian education for their children. But others were there because their parents didn't want them to go to school with African-Americans. One of my classmates—a sweet, quiet girl named Lisa—gave a speech in our social studies class on why the Ku Klux Klan was a misunderstood organization that had actually done a lot of good throughout the South. Then she smiled and sat down. For me at least, the IRS controversy has always been clarified by this one horrible speech.

Lisa's candor was matched by George Andrews, a congressman from Alabama, whose response to the 1962 Supreme Court decision was especially revealing. "They put the Negroes in the school," he said, "and now they've driven God out." By linking these two matters so crudely, Congressman Andrews was putting his finger on the real issue that reverberated throughout the South: The federal government was forcing its secular values down the throat of good Christian people. This was a region, after all, whose view of the federal government was still being shaped a century later by the memory of the Civil War. However, the first response of Christian Southerners was not to organize political resistance to federal policy but to retreat into fundamentalist communities. What led them, a decade and a half later, to change strategies so dramatically? Here's where Weyrich's claim is stunning: The threat to these communities, more than any specific moral issue like *Roe v. Wade*, galvanized fundamentalists throughout the South to take up political arms and fight.

The story Weyrich tells about private schools and the IRS is intriguing—and a little troubling—as it puts a self-interested spin on the rise of the Religious Right. The federal government was the great enemy, forcing desegregation upon the South, forcing its federal tax code on our schools. Always in the South this opposition to the federal government was tinged with the old cultural animosities that went back to the Civil War. Reagan would be the one to pull these themes together. During the years between his failed presidential campaign in 1976 and his victory in 1980, Reagan maintained a high profile and gained a loyal following. His message of small government, low taxes, and a less intrusive federal bureaucracy was heard daily in radio commentaries broadcast on several hundred stations across the nation. It was a message that resonated in the Southern states that had voted for Strom Thurmond and George Wallace. Reagan's bona fides with the new cultural conservatives was matched by his credentials with the old guard. He was the staunch anti-Communist who would follow the path Barry Goldwater had blazed a decade before.

Political pundits had greatly underestimated the potency of this combination. The conventional wisdom held that Reagan was an inherently flawed national candidate—the one Republican Jimmy Carter most wanted to face. Who could forget how Barry Goldwater in 1964 was branded a trigger-happy ideologue who couldn't be trusted with a nuclear arsenal? A columnist for the *Globe and Mail* described the Reagan nomination as "political suicide" in this analysis written in March 1980: "Mr. Reagan would lose by 2–1," he wrote. "The former California governor would be the Barry Goldwater of 1980. He is too right-wing to appeal to enough moderates to win and he is too prone to incredible gaffes." This was a widespread view among the political establishment, but the 1980 election would witness one of the most spectacular failures of political wisdom. The unelectable Reagan won in a landslide. His coattails were even long enough to pull the Senate into the Republican column for the first time in twenty-five years. Certainly the pundits had misgauged the therapeutic appeal of Reagan's optimism, coming as it did at the end of a really bad decade. But they also failed to recognize the political viability of a grassroots movement that was coalescing in the 1970s. The Moral

Majority emerged as the most visible evidence that evangelicals had crossed the political Rubicon and were ready to be political players for the first time since Prohibition.

In 1979, Paul Weyrich traveled to Lynchburg, Virginia, along with fellow activists Howard Phillips and Richard Viguerie, to meet with Jerry Falwell and lay the groundwork for the new movement. Falwell related in his autobiography that he, like other fundamentalists of his generation, had been reluctant at first to venture into politics. As the son of a bootlegger, Falwell knew how ineffective the temperance movement had been in changing the culture. Political strength had led to dramatic change—no less than an amendment to the U.S. Constitution, which is something the new conservative movement has not yet been able to match. But the law was widely unpopular and virtually unenforceable. Prohibition led to organized crime and creative new uses for bathtubs. It also led ultimately to NASCAR, as bootleggers souped up their vehicles to outrun federal agents on the back roads of the rural South. Prohibition also gave fundamentalists a black eye. So, too, did the 1925 "Scopes Monkey Trial" in Tennessee over the teaching of evolution. As the 1970s progressed, however, Falwell became convinced that Bible-believing pastors must address moral decline in America. In that decisive conversation in Lynchburg, Weyrich used the phrase "moral majority" for the first time. Falwell instinctively recognized the power of the phrase. "If we get involved," Falwell said, "that's the name of the organization." The Moral Majority would be committed to a "pro-life, pro-traditional family, pro-moral and pro-American" agenda—which was pretty much the same platform Ronald Reagan had been running on for four years. The movement had met the man.

What the Moral Majority lacked in political sophistication, it made up for in sheer energy. Like an old-time circuit preacher, Falwell barnstormed the country staging "I Love America" rallies. The rallies were old-fashioned and nostalgic, and it was easy for Falwell's critics to dismiss them as political theater. Weyrich had envisioned a finely oiled machine that could mobilize millions of voters behind core conservative policies. What he got was a traveling revival service. The rallies debuted in Richmond, Virginia, on September 13, 1979, and the first reviews in the mainstream press were little more than sneering put-downs. In an article that was unrelentingly patronizing, *Time* described Falwell as "the hyperactive founder and director of a religious empire" and the "star" of a production that was "Fourth of July inspiring." Falwell's constituency was described as "overwhelmingly white and heavy with farmers, blue-collar workers and small businessmen." A racial theme runs throughout the piece—a telling detail, as this theme would become, by the end of the decade, the principal weapon wielded by the Left against the New Right.

The lasting legacy of Falwell's entrance into national politics would not be the elections that were won or the policies that were enacted. Falwell helped to validate an evangelical Christian voice within the political system, and once all the controversial moments in his career are stripped away, that's how he should be remembered as a political figure. Christians may debate where the boundary line falls between pulpits and voting booths, but the age-old tradition that Christians must speak to the moral issues of their day had been decisively reaffirmed.

That year I proudly cast my first vote as an eighteen-year-old for Ronald Reagan. Christians like me all across America had high hopes for the changes that had come over Washington. We believed that more would come from the ballot box than the usual office shuffle as one team of bureaucrats replaced another.

The next few months would show just how wrong we were.

WHO LOST REAGAN?

The weeks between the election and inauguration of a new president always give an early read on the shape of things to come. What emerged in the winter of 1980 was an inner cabinet of California cronies and pragmatic, old-establishment Republicans. Few evangelicals were tapped for top-level positions. One of the few encouraging signs was the appointment of Dr. C. Everett Koop to the previously obscure position of surgeon general. Dr. Koop was well known among evangelicals through his collaboration with Christian apologist Francis Schaeffer on a pro-life book and film, *Whatever Happened to the Human Race?* Surely this offered a crucial opportunity to translate evangelical values into material political gains. Liberals certainly thought so and mounted a vigorous confirmation battle that Dr. Koop eventually survived. Conservatives were confident, though, that the soft-spoken doctor and devout Presbyterian would, in the end, advance their cause.

But that's not what Dr. Koop is remembered for. Early into his tenure, the surgeon general made it clear that he would not use his office as a bully pulpit to advance a pro-life agenda. To many evangelicals it began to look as though Koop was overly concerned about proving his liberal critics wrong. Or had they just misread him in the first place? When AIDS broke into the national consciousness in the early 1980s, the question was quickly resolved. Koop was less a moralist than a pragmatist. He approached the epidemic as a health issue, not an ideological battlefield, and his liberal opponents soon became his biggest fans. Koop even took pains to distance himself from the rhetoric of religious conservatives who seemed to view AIDS as an opportunity to drive home their message about moral decline in America. Yes, morality was declining in America. And yes, the AIDS crisis was driven by a subculture of promiscuity and anonymous sex. But people were also dying. Religious conservatives never found the right balance between righteous condemnation and the message of God's grace, forgiveness, and compassion.

This would be the first great defeat of the Religious Right—a defeat not so much in public policy as in public opinion. An unflattering view of conservative Christianity was being shaped at the intersection of rhetoric and policy. After years in the political wilderness, evangelicals were politically naive. They underestimated the hard rules of the game. They forgot that their political opponents would be looking to define them in the public eye before they got the chance to define themselves. The morality promoted by the Religious Right was caricatured as harsh and uncompassionate, quick to condemn and slow to love. Evangelical Christians appeared to be more concerned with scoring moral points than saving lives. Meanwhile, the "homosexual community" would emerge from the controversy as sympathetic victims. It is perversely ironic that the AIDS crisis allowed activists to repackage the "gay lifestyle" as a mainstream alternative, when that very lifestyle—with its bathhouses and cruising bars—had done so much to worsen the crisis in the first place. The relabeling of right and wrong gained traction because the public proved to be less interested in moral condemnations of homosexuality than in addressing a present health crisis. Pragmatism had triumphed, as it would time and again during the Reagan years.

Early into the Reagan presidency, it became clear that image would trump substance. Surprisingly, though, evangelicals seemed willing to accept that. When Reagan did the unthinkable and fired over eleven thousand striking air traffic controllers, evangelicals were among those who cheered his no-nonsense approach to government. And when he took a bullet in the chest and nearly died, Reagan acquired heroic status. It was hard to criticize a man who could joke about "not ducking" while being wheeled into surgery. Evangelicals would become principal custodians of the lore and legend of Ronald Reagan—the man who wanted to shrink government and restrict abortion but who was thwarted time and again by an obstinate Congress. The truth is that Reagan passed up some golden opportunities to invest his political capital in the social and moral issues that drove evangelicals to support him in the first place.

One of these opportunities came in 1981 when a vacancy opened up on the Supreme Court. Evangelicals knew what was at stake. One choice— one careful choice—and the balance of the high court would be shifted for a generation. Reagan, however, followed a different set of priorities. As a candidate he had promised to nominate the first woman to the Supreme Court, even though the pool of qualified conservative women was rather limited. The selection of Sandra Day O'Connor puzzled evangelicals, as her political record was clearly to the left of Reagan's core constituency. As a state senator, O'Connor had supported the Equal Rights Amendment and the legalization of abortion. Nevertheless, Reagan asked his supporters to sit on their hands and allow the process to play itself out. After all, O'Connor came from Senator Barry Goldwater's home state of Arizona, and she enjoyed his complete support. But even the endorsement of Mr. Conservative wasn't enough for evangelicals. When Falwell publicly questioned whether "good Christians" could get behind the O'Connor nomination, Senator Goldwater responded with a vulgar retort. The split between the old guard and the New Right was never more clear. But the record now shows that Falwell was right and Goldwater was wrong. When O'Connor retired in 2006, her praises were sung most loudly by liberal activists, feminists, and law school academics. Conservatives, on the other hand, always viewed O'Connor's confirmation as the really big fish that got away. Reagan had fulfilled a campaign promise: He nominated a woman to the high court. But he also undermined the promise he'd made to the Religious Right to work vigorously to overturn *Roe v. Wade.*

Tangible victories were hard to find on the legislative front as well. Right from the start, evangelicals were at odds with the Reagan administration over its political priorities; and right from the start, Reagan asked for patience. When Congress convened in 1981, Senate majority leader Howard Baker announced (in conjunction with the White House) that the conservative social agenda would be dealt with later—once the economy was under control. But "later" never came. A steep recession, a sharp military buildup, the global challenge of facing down the "evil empire," a campaign for reelection—all these required considerable political capital. Another election came and went, and evangelicals could not yet point to any substantive achievement. Conservatives held out hope that Reagan would push their social agenda in his second term, but that never materialized either. Reagan's 1984 landslide was so huge it blunted any talk that the Religious Right had been a decisive factor. As Reagan's time in office began to wind down, the Iran-Contra scandal brought the political machinery of Washington to a standstill. Reagan turned instead to foreign affairs, delivering his famous speech in Berlin ("Mr. Gorbachev, tear down this wall!") and negotiating arms control with the Soviet Union. The Gipper left office as a beloved figure among evangelicals, but he had fallen far short of their expectations.

How much did the Religious Right contribute to Reagan's election in 1980? Certainly evangelicals were quick to capitalize on the perception that their entrance into politics that year had been decisive. But was this true? The scale and breadth of Reagan's victory in 1980 calls that assumption into doubt. Reagan was already an established political figure when he ran for president in 1980, having fallen just short of seizing the nomination from a sitting president four years earlier. Reagan, a two-term governor of the most populous state in the country, had maintained a high public profile through radio and newspaper commentaries. Religious conservatives were just one of many demographic groups embracing Reagan's optimism that year.

Still, Reagan's victory lives on in the mythology of the Religious Right. As early as 1982, however, persuasive arguments were raised against this "election scenario." Two eminent social historians, Seymour Martin Lipset and Earl Raab, analyzed the election data and concluded that "the political strength of organizations like the Moral Majority" had been seriously overrated. The authors were writing from the unfriendly perspective of their liberal academic backgrounds. In the politically charged environment of the early Reagan years, it was easy to dismiss their judgments as tainted by partisan interest. In fact, their article was published in a book whose title lacked any subtlety whatsoever: *Speak Out against the New Right*. But a generation later, Lipset and Raab's conclusions look prophetic:

> The Americans who "turned Right" in the last election [1980] did not by any means agree with the Moral Majority or New Right programs. These Americans were not supporting specific political solutions any more than they usually do. They wanted a government that would more demonstrably reflect their mood: a more assertive America on the world scene, and on the domestic front a serious campaign to fight inflation and refurbish American industry. That is the extent of their political conservatism.

The unflattering conclusion reached by Lipset and Raab is that voters are self-interested, materialistic, and pragmatic, which shouldn't surprise us in the least. The authors went on to argue that the 1980 voters were therefore not "captive to any political movement" but were "shopping." The eventual decline of the Religious Right and the success of Bill Clinton in the 1990s largely validated these claims.

Lipset and Raab's article was prophetic in other ways too. The direction that liberal counter-attacks would take later in the decade is all too apparent in the way the authors casually introduced racial politics into the equation. The New Right, they wrote, "recalls groups like the clergymen affiliated with the Ku Klux Klan in the 1920s." They hastened to add that "today's evangelical groups have made it a point to avoid this kind of hatemongering," but this concession hardly lessened the damage caused by gratuitously dropping the KKK into their analysis. The association between religious conservatives and the dark underside of post–Civil War Southern society would remain a fruitful field for liberal partisans to plow. Many years later, Senator John McCain would even tap into that rhetoric when he described religious figures like Falwell as "agents of intolerance." It was an old, worn-out slur by the time he used it in the 2000 campaign, but it still worked its magic. McCain became the darling (for a while anyway) of the mainstream media. He was every liberal's favorite Republican because he knew how to speak the race-conscious language of the political Left.

By the end of Reagan's tenure, racial rhetoric would be the dominant weapon used against religious conservatives. In the late 1980s, the political campaigns of white supremacist David Duke would only make things worse. The racial theme would reach its culmination, however, in the failed nomination of Robert Bork to the U.S. Supreme Court. Liberal activists such as Common Cause (a group specifically mentioned a decade earlier by Falwell as one of his main reasons for founding the Moral Majority) spearheaded the opposition to the man they claimed would "turn back the clock" on civil rights. Unfortunately, the murky prehistory of the Religious Right, with its roots in the old segregationist South, only made the liberal race-baiting more effective.

Who lost Reagan? It would be wrong to see the movement's failure during the Reagan years as merely tactical. But this is exactly the assumption that Paul Weyrich has always made. In Weyrich's alternate time line, conservative Christians could have achieved material success in the early Reagan years if they had held the president's political feet to the fire. Instead, evangelicals opted for political *access* when political *success* was theirs for the taking. They were content with holding a seat at the table, as Weyrich saw it, rather than securing real legislative victories. Weyrich's critique has some merit, but it's also the convenient analysis of a man who has long held that the moral battles of our day could be won through the instruments of power and persuasion. The Moral Majority never grew into the kind of grassroots powerhouse that Weyrich had envisioned. By 1986 the name that had achieved so much notoriety, Moral Majority, was abandoned, and the organization was renamed the Liberty Foundation. In 1989 the Liberty Foundation was disbanded altogether.

A FLAWED CRUSADE

Meanwhile, as the Reagan years were winding down, I turned away from politics completely, opting instead to study dead cultures and dead languages at the University of Minnesota. In the summer of 1987 I was far from the political turmoil that dominated headlines back home. I was in Salzburg, Austria, studying German along with a diverse collection of Americans and Canadians. Most of us were knocking out language requirements for various degrees, all except for one man who seemed out of his element. David wasn't a student—not, at least, in the traditional sense. We didn't know exactly who he was, as he didn't talk much about himself. He had a lot to say, however, about Jewish conspiracies and why the Holocaust never happened.

A fellow student in the language institute took me aside one day after sizing David up for a week or so. "I have the feeling," she said, "that I've seen this guy before."

"Oh? Where?"

"In a documentary. *A documentary on the Ku Klux Klan.*"

"You're kidding," I said. But of course she wouldn't be kidding about *that.* I didn't think any more about it until a few months later, back in the States, when the former Grand Wizard of the Ku Klux Klan, David Duke, ran for political office in Louisiana and attracted national attention. I remembered the face on the television screen. This was the oddly ill-at-ease man I had repeatedly defeated at table tennis in the Alpine city where *The Sound of Music* was filmed.

David Duke was a gift to the American Left, a windfall of propaganda. Liberals learned to pounce on every coincidence of interest (however slight) between Duke and religious conservatives. Any echo in the rhetoric, and certainly any overlap in their constituencies, became one more opportunity to brand evangelicals as white supremacists in church clothes. Of course, the attacks were unfair—a form of demagoguery. But that's politics, and those who play the political game should know that their political opponents are going to hit hard. They should expect every skeleton in their closet to come out, which just might include the sad segregationist history of the church in the Old South. It's the nature of politics to deceive and distort, because politics is all about the struggle for power. Carnal instincts bring out carnal methods—and therein lies the great danger of trying to accomplish God's work through political means.

The movement was only a decade old but was already transitioning into its second fateful period that would see the rise and fall of the Christian Coalition. Where the strategy of the Moral Majority had been to rally pastors to the cause, the Christian Coalition sought to create a sophisticated and permanent political machine. This opportunity came when Pat Robertson ran for president in 1988. Long a familiar, if controversial, figure among evangelicals, Robertson claimed that God had told him to run. The affable television personality was known to millions as the host of *The 700*

Club. Only two hundred miles of tobacco fields and peanut fields separated the Robertson and Falwell ministries, but they were light-years away from each other in personality and background. Falwell was the son of a boot-legger and the graduate of a small Midwestern Bible college. Robertson was the son of a U.S. senator and a graduate of Yale Law School. As Falwell began to withdraw from his public role and focus increasingly on building Liberty University, Robertson stepped onto the stage. And there was no bigger stage than running for president.

In the Iowa caucuses in 1988, Robertson stunned Vice President George Bush, placing just ahead of him to take second place. The lead in the *New York Times* article noted that "Pat Robertson has made clear that he cannot be written off as an electronic Elmer Gantry, a color-ful distraction from the rest of the Republican Presidential field." But after some early success and enthusiasm, Robertson's campaign failed to sustain itself beyond the early contest in New Hampshire. It had been a flawed crusade, but it would end up reinventing the Religious Right in the 1990s. From the ruins of Robertson's campaign would come new life, new strategies, and a new face—the boyish face of a political whiz kid.

Ralph Reed was a twenty-nine-year-old activist when he was hired to run the new organization founded on the mailing list of the Robertson for President committee. It wouldn't take long for Reed to gain his repu-tation as the boy wonder of the Religious Right. He wasn't shy about his intentions either. "What Christians have got to do," Reed boldly told the *Los Angeles Times* in 1990, "is take back this country, one precinct at a time, one neighborhood at a time and one state at a time. I honestly believe that in my lifetime, we will see a country once again governed by Christians . . . and Christian values." Reed was underscoring the strategic shift destined to transform the movement in the post–Moral Majority years. Reed was a professional operative, not an evangelist, and he wanted to build a state-of-the-art grassroots organization. There would be no "I Love America" rallies on his agenda.

The Christian Coalition achieved some quick political successes, especially in North Carolina, where the distribution of nearly a million voter guides was widely credited with helping Senator Jesse Helms eke out a narrow reelection victory in 1990 over Charlotte mayor Harvey Gantt. This was the same Harvey Gantt who had been admitted, under court order, to Clemson University in 1962. Reed's reputation as a political tactician was cemented in Republican quarters with the Helms victory. Money flowed into the organization. Its membership swelled as new chapters opened up across the country. The party establishment was happy to use the Christian Coalition as a subcontractor in difficult races like the Helms reelection campaign. And all the while, Ralph Reed touted his new take-no-prisoners strategy.

Reed's critics have pointed to a disturbing theme of hubris that runs through the comments and strategies of the youthful political operative. One of Reed's methods, for example, was to encourage conservative candidates to take a bait-and-switch approach to selling themselves to the voters. Popular positions on taxes, for example, could mask a less popular social agenda that the public might never buy. In this way, the public would get what was best for them whether they realized it or not. This is the same hypocrisy, of course, that conservatives had long decried in candidates who ran campaigns on the values of Main Street but ended up governing like an elite ruling class.

In one of his most peculiar self-descriptions, Reed described his political tactics as those of a Turkish assassin with a long knife. "I paint my face and travel at night," he said. "You don't know it's over until you're in a body bag. You don't know until election night." In Jesus' day, the people who painted their faces and traveled at night were called *zealots*, the guerrilla warriors (another one of Ralph Reed's favorite terms) who were trying to overthrow the kingdom of Rome. Jesus certainly recruited disciples from their ranks (Simon the Zealot), but He taught them a different way to change the world. We are not to "travel at night" and conquer the world at the ballot box; we are to let our light so shine before men, that they may see our good works and glorify our Father who is in heaven (see Matthew 5:16).

The Christian Coalition was at its height after the "Contract with America" election of 1994. As the Moral Majority had done in 1980, the Christian Coalition was quick to claim a role in the dramatic shift of power as Republicans took over Congress for the first time in forty years. The Religious Right had many new friends in Washington, but once again the congressional leadership put social reform on the back burner behind government reform, tort reform, and economic reform. Once again, the movement had failed to deliver. It was 1981 all over again as conservative Christians were told to take a number and wait. Ten years later the pattern would play itself out one more time when so-called values voters in 2004 were widely credited with turning an election around for conservative candidates. "Now comes the revolution," Richard Viguerie wrote in a memorandum to conservative activists in November 2004. "If you don't implement a conservative agenda now, when do you?" But once again, despite some early optimism that Congress and the president would push an initiative on marriage, nothing happened. More pressing issues, such as the Iraq War, crowded out the social agenda.

By the time Bill Clinton's presidency was nearing its end, the Christian Coalition had ceased to be an effective advocate for conservative religious values. Many factors—some internal, some external—had contributed to the movement's stunning collapse. Reed's stealth tactics had become self-defeating, and the organization lost credibility with its own evangelical base. President Clinton had regrouped and won reelection decisively in

1996. The election was a fiasco for the Christian Coalition, as it exposed the movement's inability to affect anything but razor-thin elections. In Clinton's second term, evangelical leaders publicly supported the articles of impeachment drawn up against the president, and they paid the price of a public backlash. Clinton survived, and the Religious Right ended up looking vindictive, mean spirited, and ineffectual.

In retrospect, the Clinton years (1993–2001) underscored the fallacy that there is a "moral majority" in America. Where Carter was moral and incompetent, Clinton was immoral and politically competent. Americans chose competence with Clinton, buying into the "we can do better" rhetoric of his 1992 campaign. Where Carter had been tone deaf to the political currents around him, Clinton brought a virtuosity to the White House that has seldom been equaled. Basing policy positions on focus groups and opinion polls was ideally suited to a cynical public that valued materialism over morality. Wasn't this in some small way what the Christian Coalition had done as well? Wasn't Clinton just better at the political game?

In 1997 Ralph Reed left the Christian Coalition, and within a year the organization largely collapsed. Reed had once claimed that he wanted the Christian Coalition to become "the most powerful political organization of its kind by the year 2000." He fell considerably short of the mark. In many ways, Reed was the personification of all that went wrong with the Religious Right as it entered its second decade. With the pursuit of political success came compromise, arrogance, and even deception. Trade-offs and compromise are the language of politics, not the language of faith. Christians are to bring clarity, not nuance, to the central spiritual issues that confront humankind.

In the presidential campaign of 2000 there was no Moral Majority and no Christian Coalition. But there was Gary Bauer. Well known to evangelicals, Bauer was the former undersecretary of education in the Reagan administration and director of the Family Research Council. Like Pat Robertson before him, Bauer campaigned hard in the Iowa caucuses and the New Hampshire primary. He garnered 9 percent of the vote in Iowa and one percent in New Hampshire. Days before the primary vote, Gary Bauer appeared at one of those quirky events that are staged every four years in New Hampshire: the Bisquick Pancake Presidential Primary Flip-Off. While tossing a pancake high in the air, Bauer reached too far with his griddle and tumbled off the stage. It was an embarrassing moment, caught on video and endlessly replayed, but it was also a fitting metaphor for a movement that had reached too far. Appearing at the same event, Texas governor George W. Bush caught all his pancakes.

What would be the future of the movement at the turn of the millennium?

Focus on the Family rose to prominence among the traditional elements of the Religious Right, but new voices were raised as well. The growth of the Internet in the late 1990s meant that the movement was destined (like every other political movement) to become more and more decentralized as new voices competed with old on Web sites and blogs. Rod Dreher, a conservative columnist for the *Dallas Morning News*, has noted that "younger evangelicals are looking for something different [now]. They are not embracing their parents' view. They are looking for fresh thinking" on the future of conservativism in America. The movement had evolved well beyond the 1970s when the mailing list of the Old-Time Gospel Hour was the nerve center of the New Right and rallies on state capitols were its chief strategy.

A BROKEN REED

What happened to the man who vowed to take back America one precinct at a time? At the biblical age of thirty-three, Ralph Reed had become a *Time* magazine cover with a headline that read, "The Right Hand of God." As director of the Christian Coalition, he was at the top of his influence after the political earthquake of 1994 brought a Republican Congress to Washington. Within a few years, Reed would leave a shrinking organization, return to Georgia as a political consultant, and begin plotting his own entry into politics. The race for lieutenant governor in 2006 was to be the first of many steps into the political ring, perhaps one day even leading to the White House. Early in the race for the Republican nomination, Reed was outpacing his lesser-known opponent in opinion polls, fund-raising, and organization. And then the wheels came off. Reed lost the nomination by 12 percent.

The morning after Reed's primary defeat, the *New York Times* could hardly contain its glee, judging from how much they managed to pack into the lead sentence:

> Ralph Reed, the former director of the Christian Coalition and a former Republican lobbyist involved in the Jack Abramoff scandal, suffered an embarrassing defeat in his effort to win the Republican nomination for lieutenant governor on Tuesday.

As the *Times* was quick to point out, the most "embarrassing" reason for Reed's collapse was his connection to superlobbyist Jack Abramoff, who pleaded guilty in January 2006 to influence peddling. Before the year was out, candidates in both parties who had been associated with Abramoff, including Ralph Reed, had been dragged down to defeat. Some were found guilty of wrongdoing, such as Representative Bob Ney of Ohio, but most of the politicians caught up in the scandal were tainted by association. It was electoral poison just to have met with Abramoff and taken campaign money from his interests, even if no laws had been violated. The Abramoff scandal focused the national spotlight on money and corruption in American politics, but it also exposed the tragic compromises that conservative politicians and evangelical leaders like Reed had been willing to make in pursuit of their own careers.

The connection between Abramoff and Reed surprised many, but their friendship actually extended back into their college years, when both were active as College Republicans. Later, when Reed left the Christian Coalition and established his own consulting firm in Atlanta, Abramoff became one of the first contacts in a growing Rolodex file— and not just because his last name starts with *A*. "Hey, now that I'm done with electoral politics," Reed wrote to Abramoff in an e-mail, "I need to start humping in corporate accounts! I'm counting on you to help me with some contacts." The trade-off would involve "3,000 pastors and 90,000 religious conservative households" in Alabama that Reed could mobilize for a retainer fee of $20,000 per month—all in an effort to defeat a state lottery initiative. It seemed a natural fit for Reed to tap into the old networks of the Christian Coalition to defeat a gambling measure.

But Abramoff was no moral crusader. Behind the public campaign lay another agenda. Abramoff wanted the state lottery defeated because it would compete directly with the gambling monopoly that his client, the Choctaw Indian tribe, held in the state. The tribe stood to lose millions if Alabamans started lining up at their neighborhood 7-Eleven to buy lotto tickets instead of visiting the Indian casinos. Without knowing it, the ordinary voters on Reed's mailing list had joined a game of political blackjack—and they were being rolled. Evangelical voters had been enlisted in the noble cause of helping one gambling interest neutralize another. The tactic was a classic bait-and-switch, the product of behind-the-scenes calculations that evangelical voters never endorsed. No illegalities were ever alleged, but Reed had undermined his credibility with his own base—a fatal political mistake. Ironically, this is the same path of compromise that Reed had taken the Christian Coalition down in the 1990s, when he encouraged conservative candidates to soft-pedal their social agendas and play up their more popular positions on taxes and government waste. One can understand the sense of disillusionment and even betrayal that many felt when the Reed-Abramoff connection was fleshed out in media outlets that had always been hostile to evangelicals. Reed had handed his enemies the one weapon they could never forge for themselves—the hypocrisy of the movement.

In his defense, Reed claimed not to have known that the 4 million dollars directed by Abramoff toward Reed's consulting firm was "gambling money." But this is exactly the kind of thing that Reed, with his reputation as a micromanager and a savvy operative, might be expected to know. Predictably, his opponent for the Republican nomination, state senator Casey Cagle, pointed out the inconsistency in a devastating series of ads. Reed had called gambling immoral, Cagle reminded voters, but then accepted thousands of dollars from the Indian casino industry. The Religious Right had traveled a long road from defending the rights of the unborn to defending the right of the Choctaw Indian tribe to maintain a gambling monopoly.

☆

The rise and fall of Ralph Reed should be a cautionary tale for evangelicals, teaching us that the mixture of politics, religion, money, and influence leads inevitably to compromise. The movement that had sought to speak the truth fearlessly to its generation ended up compromising its message, its methods, and its mission. One historian has written that the Christian Right experienced early political success when it "learned to engage the world." And how did it do this? The movement "learned to engage the world *because it has become more like the world.*" This is a sad, but inevitable, commentary on a failed political movement. How could it have been otherwise? Jesus told us plainly that what "is highly esteemed among men is an abomination in the sight of God" (Luke 16:15). In this passage, Jesus was denouncing the arrogance of the Pharisees, who were the guardians of public morality in their day. "No servant can serve two masters," Jesus also said, "for either he will hate the one, and love the other; or else he will hold to the one, and despise the other" (Luke 16:13, kjv).

What we need as evangelical Christians is a radical reassessment of our core cultural values—the kind that Jesus brought to the legalistic Judaism of His day, the kind that early Roman Christians brought to the pagan, materialistic culture of Rome. Evangelicals need to assess how much of the world's values we've absorbed and turned into public extensions of our theology. Certainly, the rise of evangelical activism has been motivated in part by righteous anger, but it's also been driven by the cultural fear of "losing" America. Evangelicals must come to terms with our failure to effect substantive change within American society, our failure to prevent a further slide into a post-Christian future. What accounts for this failure? The answer lies, I believe, in a defective view of the past and a compromised view of the church's role within society. As we look toward the future, I trust that "success" for Christians in the public arena will be gauged by our faithfulness to the truth, not by specific victories at the ballot box or in the courtroom. We've allowed our standard of success to be dictated by a whole set of assumptions that come from the culture around us, not from the Word of God. For millions of believers, the distinction between what is "Christian" and what is "American" has become hopelessly blurred—which is why we must turn next to the controversial question of America's Christian heritage.

CHAPTER TWO

How Christian a Nation?

Even though America once had a Christian orientation, we are now living in an era we could call post-Christian America.

— JOHN F. MACARTHUR

You used to live here?" my wife asked as we drove through the peach orchards and cotton fields in the blazing heat of a summer day.

I was returning to Hartsville, South Carolina, some thirty years after arriving there as a confused fourteen-year-old boy fresh from the jungles of Central Africa. I never thought I'd go back. I never wanted to. But something happens when you hit middle age, and people you haven't seen for decades start coming to mind. *I wonder what she looks like now. I wonder what he made of his life. I wonder—*

Janel was waiting for my response. "You used to live *here*?" she asked again.

"What do you mean?" I said. "This is *Gawd's* country." There was a gently mocking tone to my voice. I had learned as a teenager that this phrase, *God's country*, was a common idiom in the South, used in a joking way, usually as a way of distinguishing the South from the North, or Clemson football country from, say, Georgia football country.

"God's country? There's nothing here!" said Janel. She'd grown up in Southern California.

"Wait till I take you to the Piggly Wiggly."

"The what?"

"The Piggy Wiggly. It's a grocery store with a smiling pig for a logo where you can get fresh collard greens and black-eyed peas. . . ."

Janel rolled her eyes as if to say, "I can hardly wait."

Hartsville had changed, of course, like small towns all across America. That blanket of sameness that has spread over the American continent had reached here, too. There was a Wal-Mart now on the outskirts of town, and the usual fast-food restaurants were everywhere. The black high school had been closed for many years, and the building now stood in ruins. But there was still a "black section" of town, and it remained dreadfully poor. And on the other side of town there were still grand old homes with stately trees.

Hartsville had changed—but so had I.

I no longer believed there was such a place as "God's country." Not on earth, anyway. Not since the time of the prophets and kings of ancient Israel. Sure, we use that expression in a lighthearted way to express our regional pride, *but we also mean it.* When we say that America is a Christian nation, we're really claiming in fairly crude terms that it's God's country.

Is that true? Is America God's country? Was our nation established "under God"? The default answer for many evangelicals has been yes. The answer comes easily, almost automatically, especially when you look at our prosperity, our industrial might among the nations, our rapid rise to political power and influence. When you cross-reference the answer with some well-chosen quotations, such as Alexis de Tocqueville's "America is great because America is good," and throw into the mix America's support for Israel, then you seem to have made a compelling case indeed. But what does our history really tell us? And more important, what does the Scripture say? These are necessary questions to confront, no matter how uncomfortable they make us, since we've grounded so much political theology on the uncertain foundation of our Christian heritage.

THE HISTORICAL ANSWER

Millions of Americans were outraged in the summer of 2002 when the Ninth Circuit Court of Appeals, the most liberal court in America by most accounts, ruled that it was unconstitutional to require students in public schools to recite the Pledge of Allegiance. Self-professed atheist Michael Newdow had argued that the phrase "under God" violated the separation of church and state and was a terrible imposition on his young daughter. The court agreed, noting in its ruling that the 1954 law that had enshrined the phrase into the Pledge of Allegiance was meant "to recognize a Supreme Being" at a time "when the government was publicly inveighing against atheistic Communism." The court also took note of what President Dwight Eisenhower had affirmed when he signed the law into effect: "From this day forward, the millions of our school children will daily proclaim in every city and town, every village and rural school-house, the dedication of our Nation and our people to the Almighty."

The political reaction was swift and predictable. Before the day was out, a hundred congressmen, mostly Republicans, staged a publicity stunt by gathering on the steps of the U.S. Capitol to recite the Pledge of Allegiance in unison. The Newdow case exposed so many contradictions, so much self-interest, and so many ironies. It's ironic, for instance, that the most liberal court in the land actually took into account the "original intent" of the law as expressed by the words of President Eisenhower. Liberal jurists are often contemptuous of "strict constructionists" who place great importance on the original intent behind the Constitution. There is plenty of collateral evidence that judges *could* rely on, if they were so inclined, that would put a different spin on their rulings about

God, life, liberty, and happiness. On the other side of the bench, it is just as ironic that federal attorneys defended the Pledge in court by arguing that it conveyed minimal religious content and was merely an expression. In other words, the government was arguing that the phrase conservatives were so passionate in defending should be preserved *because it really means nothing at all!*

☆

So, what does the phrase "under God" really mean? In 1863 Abraham Lincoln stood on a wooden platform under a gray November sky and used this very phrase at Gettysburg. Since Lincoln introduced these words into our political vocabulary, it makes sense to consider carefully what he said and (more important) what he meant. Certainly Lincoln had no idea that these words would become controversial. Where would the controversy lie, after all, if the meaning of the phrase is self-evident? It's tempting to conclude, then, that we've found irrefutable evidence that one of our greatest presidents considered us to be a Christian nation in the sense that evangelicals today understand.

But history is never that easy.

Three reporters transcribed Lincoln's 1863 speech in shorthand and telegraphed the contents to their newspaper offices. The president's words were printed the following morning in newspapers from Boston to Cincinnati. Lincoln returned to the White House and gave two handwritten copies of the speech—believed by historians to be his first and second drafts—to his personal assistants, John Nicolay and John Hay. Over the next few months, Lincoln responded to personal requests by writing out three more copies by hand, known as the Everett, Bancroft, and Bliss manuscripts.

We have, therefore, three distinct records of that memorable speech:

the two draft copies prepared before the delivery, the newspaper transcriptions of what Lincoln actually said at the ceremony, and three "autograph" copies that he later prepared upon request. There are minor stylistic changes from copy to copy as Lincoln continued to polish the wording and rhythm of the text. But one small change Lincoln made has major implications for how we understand our Christian heritage: He added the phrase "under God."

> It is rather for us to be here dedicated to the great task remaining before us—that from these honored dead we take increased devotion to that cause for which they gave the last full measure of devotion—that we here highly resolve that these dead shall not have died in vain—that this nation, under God, shall have a new birth of freedom—and that government of the people, by the people, for the people, shall not perish from the earth.

The phrase "under God" would be added to the Pledge of Allegiance in 1954 on the grounds that Lincoln had spoken these words at Gettysburg. Lincoln didn't write this phrase into his first and second drafts, however— the so-called Nicolay and Hay manuscripts. But he most likely *did* speak the words, perhaps improvising at the last minute by adding them to the reading copy he had taken from his coat pocket. All three newspaper transcriptions were rendered in stenographic shorthand while Lincoln slowly spoke, and all three agree on his wording: "This nation shall, *under God*, have a new birth of freedom." When Lincoln later polished the speech and wrote it out for Everett, Bancroft, and Bliss, he shifted the phrase in the sentence, moving it before the verb to its now familiar form: "This nation, *under God*, shall have a new birth of freedom."

Though some deny that Lincoln ever spoke these words at all, most historians agree that he did include the phrase in his spoken delivery.

There is, however, little agreement as to his reasons for adding the phrase and what he was intending to say. Some see it as a blanket endorsement of the view that America is a Christian nation. Others argue that Lincoln was employing a proverbial expression, common in the political rhetoric of the eighteenth and nineteenth centuries, an expression that means something like, "as Providence ordains it." Depending on how you read it, Lincoln was either making a strong statement of divine destiny or a weak statement of philosophical fatalism. Both positions can be well defended. Christians are naturally inclined to hear Lincoln affirming that a divine hand has guided American history. But Lincoln repeatedly confessed his fatalism to friends and family. "I have all my life been a fatalist," he told one of his congressional allies. One of his law clerks recalled how Lincoln believed "that the universe is governed by one uniform, unbroken, primordial law." Other voices can be added to the historical record, including his wife, Mary Todd Lincoln, who described Lincoln's belief that "what is to be will be, and no cares of ours can arrest or reverse the decree." The "plain" historical facts of what Lincoln said turn out to be more complex than we had hoped.

Is this nothing more than an obscure debate for historians? Hardly. More is at stake here than what was said at Gettysburg—much more than a scholarly quibble about which reading copy Lincoln took from his coat pocket. Those who read this speech in different ways are arguing about nothing less than the correct "reading copy" of American history. Are we, or are we not, a Christian nation "under God"? America has entered a new century more divided than at any time since Virginians fought New Yorkers in the fields and forests of our own continent. Our nation is once again "engaged in a great civil war," as Lincoln described it then, "testing whether that nation, or any nation so dedicated and so conceived, can long endure." This new war is being waged over the airwaves, in the courts, in our schools, and in the marketplace—not in the wheat fields of Pennsylvania or the tobacco fields of Virginia. One of the central ideas under dispute in this war of ideas is our Christian heritage, which is why many evangelical Christians have taken up this battle as their own. Unfortunately, Lincoln gives us very little guidance in this controversy.

If what Lincoln meant is unclear, then we should go back further for a historical answer to the question, all the way back to the Founding Fathers. Certainly they can settle the question for us. At least, this is the assumption of many who argue that the Founding Fathers were Bible-believing Christians whose words speak for themselves. Of course, there were a few ungodly rabble-rousers like Tom Paine and a few rakes like Ben Franklin (though even he trembled in prayer at the Constitutional Congress). But these are the exceptions that prove the rule. On balance, these were godly men—purpose-driven men, we might even say, as though we could find them worshiping comfortably at some megachurch in suburban America. Without the powdered wigs, of course.

The words of the Founding Fathers have become the primary evidence used to argue that America was *founded* as a Christian nation, under God. It's as though we can merely perform a text search on the collected works of our Founding Fathers, tabulate the number of times God is invoked, and then argue *on statistical grounds* that we're a Christian nation. We're told to just listen to what they said for themselves, since the plain sense of their words should settle the dispute once and for all. Certainly that seems to be the case when you read that John Adams and John Hancock jointly declared in 1775 that "we recognize no sovereign but God, and no king but Jesus." Or that Thomas Jefferson proclaimed himself "a real Christian, that is to say, a disciple of the doctrines of Jesus."

In a pamphlet entitled "An Examination of Our American Spiritual Heritage," one evangelical leader wrote the following:

> Given this vast volume of historical evidence, it is utterly foolish to deny that we have been, from the beginning, a people of faith whose government is built wholly on a Judeo-Christian foundation. Yet those of our people who do not study history can be duped into believing anything.

Those of us who study history—and who follow Christ—find much to be troubled about in statements like this. Such a view is deficient because it fails to distinguish between cultural Christianity and biblical Christianity. We cannot deny that our institutions and our culture, like the rest of the Western world, have been profoundly shaped by Christian values, ideas, and doctrines. But to say that our system of government "is built *wholly* on a Judeo-Christian foundation" is the kind of rhetorical overreach that secularists are guilty of on the other side of the argument.

The record is quite a bit muddier than that. Adams and Hancock were making a political statement, not a theological one, in rejecting the authority of King George. And Thomas Jefferson, who proclaimed himself "a real Christian," was conveniently selective about which doctrines of Jesus he included in his own anti-supernaturalist edition of the Bible. Like many of the Founding Fathers, Jefferson was deeply conflicted about the competing claims of revealed religion and the dictates of reason. He was a bundle of contradictions—a man who wrote that "all men are created equal" but who was quick to make exceptions for his slaves. A man who wrote to the Danbury Baptists in 1802 about a "wall of separation" between church and state, but who then attended (two days later) a church service held in the U.S. Capitol building! If we see contradictions in Jefferson's life and writings, it's because he never fully worked out the details for himself. Historians will do no better in sorting out what Jefferson left unsorted. Partisans on the Right and Left, too, cannot expect to assess fairly a man who was a cipher and a paradox, a man who prayed at public events but who had no particular expectation that God would hear him. Jefferson has become the great Rorschach test of American history: Liberals and conservatives see in him pretty much what they want to see. Both sides long to make Jefferson one of their own and draft him into their separate battles to "take back America." All the while, Jefferson is the classic fence-sitter who can't make up his mind. And herein lies the great contradiction that is America. We are at once a "Christian" nation and a nation that is the fullest expression of humanistic ideals. This is not what evangelicals normally mean, however, when they refer casually to our "religious heritage."

Despite their private questions and personal doubts, the public declarations of the Founding Fathers indicate that these men held a high view of religion in public life. Without exception, they viewed the laws of God as foundational to a civil society. None questioned that God and His laws should be reverenced in the public square. But they were also deeply suspicious of ecclesiastical power. They had every right to be; they had seen its abuses. This is why they always opted for a middle course. On the one hand, the Founding Fathers (Jefferson included) would have readily acknowledged that America is *Christian*, at least in some innocuous cultural sense. They would not have understood our raging controversies over the symbols and language of faith, since they promoted these very symbols themselves. On the other hand, they certainly did not see themselves founding a theocratic state.

Another historical problem arises when Christians defend our "spiritual heritage," as some call it. Exactly *which* people are we speaking about? Exactly *which* America do we have in mind? We cannot assume that an easy continuity runs through our history, a providential thread that links the Pilgrims, the Founding Fathers, and contemporary evangelicals. Thinking historically involves placing things in a fully rounded context, reconstructing the landscapes of meaning as best we can for the events and texts of the past. As Mark Noll reminded us in *The Scandal of the Evangelical Mind* (1994), we have too little regard—perhaps it's too little patience—for the demands history places on us. To cite any number of documents in which the Founding Fathers invoked the name of God as evidence that America was founded as a Christian nation involves an astonishingly bold leap—one that disregards rhetorical function and cultural behavior altogether.

Both sides in the culture war are able to build their all-or-nothing cases on historical evidence. But neither side is playing fair with history. The record is much less clear than the culture warriors of our day make it seem. One of the results of thinking historically about our own traditions is that we soon realize that there is not just one America but *many* Americas, both then and now. Evangelicals may want to focus on the Puritanism of the first Massachusetts settlers, but what of the leisurely life of Southern gentlemen, for whom good food, good drink, and good times were self-justifying ways of life? Secularists may want to play up the role of Enlightenment philosophy in shaping our political institutions, but what about the equally important role played by the Great Awakening? Very different Americas are apparent in the haphazard and improvised way our nation was settled. It was an idea, more than anything, that pulled the disparate elements of this nation together—the idea we call *Americanism*.

THE CULTURAL ANSWER

The idea of an *American* nation, an *American* people, an *American* destiny, began to coalesce in the decades after the Civil War. A retired president of Yale University, Theodore Woolsey, was really speaking about this emerging national identity when he asked the question in 1873, "In what sense can this country be called a Christian country?"

Woolsey is an interesting, if minor, nineteenth-century public man who prefigures many of the attributes found in the Religious Right a century later. Though he was a professor of international law, it was the intersection of morality and public policy that interested him the most. In his influential book *Divorce and Divorce Legislation* (1869), Woolsey argued that "petitions for divorce become more numerous with the ease of obtaining them." Woolsey contended that "lax divorce laws have caused the disintegration of the family." After retiring from Yale, he became a political activist and spokesman for "family values." As the president of the New England Divorce Reform League, he shepherded its growth in 1885 into a national lobbying group—the National Divorce Reform League. Woolsey also served as chairman of the American commission for the revision of the Authorized Version of the Bible and was a leader in the Evangelical Alliance. Add to this his staunch anticommunism, and Woolsey can almost be seen as a forerunner of the Moral Majority. This despite his roots in Yankee New England and Yale College.

In one significant way, however, Woolsey did *not* prefigure the Religious Right. In his carefully worded definition of America as a Christian nation, we hear no echo of destiny. Woolsey gave us no reason to believe that America is driven by a divine mandate. When given the chance, he refused to make destiny the centerpiece of his definition. He was restrained in what he would claim about our Christian heritage.

In what sense could this country be called a Christian country then? In this sense certainly: that the vast majority of the people believed in Christ and the gospel, that Christian influences were universal, and that the civilization and intellectual culture were built on that foundation.

Woolsey concisely identified three standards—demographic, cultural, and intellectual—by which America in 1873 could be called a Christian country. If we apply the same criteria to America today, however, we see how far we've progressed toward our post-Christian future. It can no longer be claimed on demographic grounds that the "vast majority" of Americans believe in Christ and the gospel. We do remain a highly religious people, especially when compared with Western Europe, but Americans are increasingly satisfying their metaphysical needs through forms of spirituality that have little or nothing to do with orthodox Christianity.

Nor are the cultural influences of Christianity any longer "universal," as Woolsey described them. Liberal activists in law, education, and the media have squeezed Christian imagery out of the courtroom, classroom, marketplace, and airwaves. This is not a surprising development; it's a process that's been underway for a long time. Still, the secularizing of American society removes a central plank from Woolsey's definition.

Woolsey's third criterion was an uncontroversial truism in 1873: "Our civilization and intellectual traditions are built on a Christian foundation." The trend in American education toward multiculturalism, however, has obscured the "Christian foundation" that Woolsey identified. The well-meaning attempt to be inclusive and diverse in our curricula has flattened out real distinctions among competing value systems and, in the process, diluted the impact Christianity has had in our history.

The ground was shifting under his feet when Woolsey spoke in 1873. This was the post–Civil War period historians call the Reconstruction, by which we narrowly mean the political, economic, and social rebuilding of the South. But it was a time when America was reconstructed, too, in ways not gauged by economic growth and political enfranchisement. America was coming of age, and out of this reconstruction would come an American mythology of our founding as a nation and our future within the world. The seeds of a new civil war—the culture war we're embroiled in today—would be sown during this period. Christianity and Americanism would become intertwined in the new mythology; by the end of this period, however, the story we tell about our nation would diverge into competing visions of America: one Christian and one secular.

Politically, we see the development of American federalism in the aftermath of the Civil War. Some have argued that Lincoln's Gettysburg Address was the preamble to the so-called second American Constitution (the series of constitutional amendments that were quickly ratified following the Civil War). New amendments were quickly ratified, and the relationship between Washington and the individual states had been altered forever. The constitutional battle over states' rights and civil rights would become a defining political reality of twentieth-century America.

Economically, America was playing catch-up with the European powers. It didn't take too long, however, for the great untapped natural resources of the continent to spur the industrialization of America and our ascendancy as an economic world power. A more aggressive federal government was well suited to the growing complexities of an industrialized nation that was busy laying down railroad tracks from coast to coast, building factories, and fighting wars in distant places.

Socially, the nation was undergoing three very different waves of migration. Catholic immigrants poured into America's cities from Ireland and Italy—socially conservative families that would become Reagan Democrats in a hundred years. African-Americans depopulated the South and migrated to Northern cities like Detroit, Chicago, St. Louis, and New York. Homesteaders like my ancestors moved westward with the frontier and helped to define the conservative ideal of American self-reliance.

Intellectually, we see the rise of modern liberalism in American culture with its roots in Darwinian materialism. The old American instinct of practicality was retooled as pragmatism, a philosophy that is ultimately anchored in the Darwinian worldview. Universities that had been founded as Christian institutions became bastions of progressive ideology. Theological liberalism became entrenched in American life as the "social gospel." Ultimately, the fundamentalist movement would emerge as a reaction to modernism in all its guises—Darwinism, pragmatism, socialism, and theological liberalism.

But we also see the *mythological* reconstruction of America. Our contemporary idea of America was "invented" during this period that saw the institution of public education spread across America. The one-room schoolhouse would evolve into a powerful bureaucracy— the great normalizing force within American society. A nation that was growing into a world power would need a cohesive public education system that could assimilate immigrants, Americanize them, and train them effectively for maximum industrial and agricultural output. In short, public schools would put to good use the new philosophy of pragmatism and the new mythology of Americanism. Christianity and Americanism were accepted in the classroom as compatible sets of values. One could salute the flag and honor the Bible, and no one imagined for a moment that the ACLU would be filing suit. We should harbor no nostalgic regrets over the loss of this easy compatibility between "Christianity" and Americanism. It was, after all, a *cultural* Christianity—not a biblical one—that served the political interests of an emerging world power.

Like Theodore Woolsey, a majority of Americans at this time were quite comfortable merging Christian values with American culture. But that would begin to change. The growing influence of Darwinian science and the demographic pressures of immigration would alter the political landscape. Eastern European Jews and Southern European Catholics were pouring into American society. For the secularist, these factors were reason to limit Protestant Christian influences in public places. For the fundamentalist, these intellectual and social developments sharpened the argument that we are a *Christian* nation—that is, a *Protestant* nation, not a Catholic or Jewish one.

Abraham Lincoln said that "we cannot escape history," and this truth is nowhere more evident in our own national history than in the movements that were spawned in the decades following the Civil War. The foundations of our national mythology were set in place—America as a land of opportunity and a nation of destiny—and these were values that Americans of all political persuasions, parties, and backgrounds could endorse. As our nation reached the early twentieth century and the threshold of the First World War, this mythology was already branching into two different directions, ones that would ulti-mately yield the culture wars of the twentieth century. A bespectacled, round-faced intellectual named Herbert Croly saw this happening as far back as 1909.

☆

Nearly a hundred years have passed since Herbert Croly, a leading turn-of-the-century progressive and founding editor of the *New Republic*, pub-lished a telling critique of American exceptionalism. In *The Promise of American Life* (1909), Croly presented an insightful critique of American values, and in the process, managed to give us a political blueprint for the ideological battles of the late twentieth century.

> The substance of our national Promise has consisted . . . of an
> improving popular economic condition, guaranteed by demo-
> cratic political institutions, and resulting in moral and social

amelioration. These manifold benefits were to be obtained merely by liberating the enlightened self-interest of the American people. The beneficent result followed inevitably from the action of wholly selfish motives—provided, of course, the democratic political system of equal rights was maintained in its integrity. The fulfillment of the American Promise was considered inevitable because it was based upon a combination of self-interest and the natural goodness of human nature. On the other hand, if the fulfillment of our national Promise can no longer be considered inevitable, it must be considered as equivalent to a conscious national purpose instead of an inexorable national destiny.

There's much to unpack in Croly's summation of the American Promise. He outlined the generic political platform of every politician: tangible improvements in the economic, political, social, and moral lives of the American citizen. In so doing, he was pointing out that American liberalism and conservatism share a common deep structure, a common mythology—a commitment to economic, political, moral, and social amelioration. But we see the critical line of divergence that would open up so wide a century later. Croly wondered "if the fulfillment of our national Promise can no longer be considered inevitable." A trust has been betrayed in that "the traditional American confidence in individual freedom has resulted in a morally and socially undesirable distribution of wealth." Still, the grand promise of America can be achieved, Croly argued, by "a conscious national purpose instead of an inexorable national destiny." Here we find in a single phrase the metaphysical divide between conservative and liberal views of America that still inform our public policy debates. Here's how Croly's two categories relate to the culture wars of our own day:

"conscious national purpose"	"inexorable national destiny"
a liberal political philosophy	a conservative political philosophy
"reality-based" community	evangelical Christians
blue states	red states

Croly can be read as the Rosetta stone of modern American liberalism. The denial of "an inexorable national destiny" (with all its metaphysical assumptions) lies at the heart of his critique of America at the beginning of what historians would come to call the "American century." At the beginning of the twenty-first century, this same denial of destiny is one of the basic worldview assumptions of those self-described members of the reality-based community. Destiny, for them, is just another spooky superstitious category of thought that enlightened people can no longer accept. Progressives occupy the *real* world of sober, rational analysis. If we are to define the future—rather than be defined by it—then we must be driven by a "conscious national purpose." The crusade led by former vice president Al Gore to combat global warming is a clear example of this progressive worldview in action. The premise of Gore's book *The Assault on Reason* (2007) has its intellectual roots in Croly's "conscious national purpose." President Bush, on the other hand, has been roundly criticized by progressive secularists for his belief in an "inexorable national destiny."

What accounts for this striking shift from Woolsey to Croly? America had traveled a long distance, but it was an inevitable journey. America has always been both religious and secular, but its secular instincts were starting to gain the upper hand. Woolsey in 1873 was still confident in his belief that America was a Christian nation. A generation later, however, Croly defined America as the product of material forces shaped by rational minds. A dividing line that was always present in our national psyche was now opening up like a fault line in our culture and politics. On the one side, a Christianized American mythology would become part of the rhetoric of religious conservatives; on the other side, a secularized mythology would come to characterize progressives, liberals, and increasingly the Democratic party. Viewed this way, the battle between religious conservatives and secular liberals in contemporary America looks more like a battle of mythologies than a battle of moralities. Both political mythologies—the Christianized and the secular—are trying to "take back America" to the way things used to be before the other side messed things up.

THE THEOLOGICAL ANSWER

For the Christian, the controversy over our religious heritage should be settled not by history or culture but by Scripture. The theological answer must begin with what the word Christian really means. Christians are individuals—not organizations or political entities. I teach at a *Christian* university, as it is commonly described, but even this is a subtle misapplication of the biblical term. More than a semantic quibble, this is a theological distinction of great importance. The radical message of the gospel—a message revived in Reformation theology—is that you and I stand before a holy God as *individuals* only because of the atoning work of Jesus Christ. We come to God not in a collective sense but through the Cross. "There is one God and one Mediator between God and men, the Man Christ Jesus" (1 Timothy 2:5). When we speak of a Christian, then, we are invoking the most profound theology of our faith and a central plank of the Reformation. A Christian is a man or woman who has been justified by Christ. Schools, mission agencies, publications—not to mention nations—just don't qualify. There's another reason why nations can't be Christian. Scripture is clear that Israel was the only nation God elected in His wisdom for a special role in the world: to be a witness of God's glory, to reveal God's holiness, to deliver God's law, and to usher the Messiah into the world. Today, God accomplishes His work in the world through the church.

So, in this biblical sense, America is not and never could have been a Christian nation. Nor has God made any provision for America, or for any other nation, to be "Christian." Nations have no standing before God any more than corporations, the local chamber of commerce, or the neighborhood glee club do. These are human institutions that serve human ends. In His sovereignty, God certainly does work through nations. But He no longer elects certain nations over others to anoint with His blessing. He works through individual believers empowered by the Holy Spirit, living by faith, and ministering in the body of Christ—the church.

We are wrong to take the words of King David out of context— "Blessed is the nation whose God is the LORD" (Psalm 33:12)—and apply them to America. But this happens every year on the third Thursday of May, when religious and community leaders around the nation gather for annual prayer breakfasts. Only half of the verse is ever quoted though. David goes on to define which nation he's talking about: "the people He has chosen as His own inheritance." This makes all the difference in the world. Israel was God's chosen people, the nation whose God was the Lord. This unique status has not passed to America or to any other earthly nation. Peter tells us instead that the church is "a chosen generation, a royal priesthood, a holy nation, His own special people" (1 Peter 2:9).

We like to see the blessing of God in our economic and military power. But when Jesus was born in Bethlehem, Caesar Augustus was the pagan emperor of Rome, and the imperial army stood unchallenged in the world. Romans saw the blessing of Jupiter on their Empire as much as we see the blessing of God. We cannot index God's favor to our national treasury any more than the ancient Romans could. If this were not true, then the emerging power of China would pose a real theological problem. Does this nation that persecutes Christians now enjoy the blessing of God?

America is not the first nation to fall under the spell of a theocratic vision. After Constantine converted to Christianity in 311, the Roman Empire embarked on its long and troubled Christian career. Some good things happened, of course. The systematic persecution of Christians came to an end. Moral laws were signed into effect by imperial decree. The gladiatorial shows were outlawed. A vigorous culture war was waged in the late fourth and early fifth century against the last vestiges of Roman paganism. In due course, however, the church became powerful, wealthy, and corrupt—and the newly Christianized Empire collapsed. As a self-styled Christian empire, Rome did not give us a promising model to follow.

Church and state became codependent once again in the early Middle Ages with the coronation of Charlemagne in 800 as "Holy Roman Emperor." Again, some good things were accomplished as culture flourished, education revived, and the biblical text was preserved through the diligent transcription of medieval monks. Some really bad things happened too, as the church became a powerful political institution. Perhaps the single worst legacy of late medieval Christianity was the Crusades—a monumental policy blunder that we're still paying for today.

Great Britain, too, at the height of its empire, saw itself as a Christian nation uniquely blessed by God. England sent the first wave of modern missionaries throughout the world and instilled a legacy of civil government in its colonies. But "Christian" England also left its colonial imprint on the reputation of the church. To this day, missionaries in India and Africa struggle against the misconception that Christianity is a Western religion, another cultural import like cricket or Coca-Cola.

If America is not a Christian nation, then this forces us to reassess the church's role in public life. Again, Scripture is clear on this point: God has not entrusted His work to a nation but to the church. Though Christians have great freedom to be engaged in every aspect of the political process, the church must stay focused on its narrow job description. Scripture has defined and delimited the church's role in very specific terms. Jesus commissioned His followers to "go therefore and make disciples of all the nations, baptizing them in the name of the Father and of the Son and of the Holy Spirit, teaching them to observe all things that I have commanded you" (Matthew 28:19-20). The church is not bound to any one nation's agenda; rather, the church transcends man-made boundaries of culture and politics. Nor has the mission of the church changed over time. Jesus punctuated the Great Commission with this reminder: "Lo, I am with you always, even to the end of the age" (Matthew 28:20, emphasis added). He is still walking in the midst of His seven golden lampstands (see Revelation 2:1), and the mandate He gave to the church will not expire until the end of the age.

The apostle Paul gave us a clear picture of the church's mission in the world. Writing to the Ephesians, he defined the church as a spiritual body, the body of Christ, called to a spiritual task:

> He Himself gave some to be apostles, some prophets, some evange-
> lists, and some pastors and teachers, for the equipping of the saints
> for the work of ministry, for the edifying of the body of Christ, till
> we all come to the unity of the faith and of the knowledge of the
> Son of God, to a perfect man, to the measure of the stature of the
> fullness of Christ. **EPHESIANS 4:11-13**

There were no precinct captains or political fund-raisers given to the church. Not even congressmen or presidents. Only apostles, prophets, evangelists, and pastor-teachers. Why? Because the twofold work of the church is to equip the saints for ministry and to build up the body of Christ. The end result should be the unity of our faith and knowledge as we become "grown-up" Christians, grounded in the Word of God and empowered by the Holy Spirit. Paul's desire is that "we should no longer be children, tossed to and fro and carried about with every wind of doctrine" (Ephesians 4:14). When Christians on either end of the political spectrum redefine the church as a voting bloc instead of Christ's very body, then we have succumbed to a false wind of doctrine.

It's easy to identify this defect in those who happen to be on the "other side" of our political position. It's less easy—and less comfortable—to see this defect in ourselves. The nostalgic Americanism of conservative culture, for example, has become so enmeshed with evangelical faith that we can no longer clearly see the boundary between the two. The church's mission is not to transform a changing culture but to bear witness to the unchanging truth of God. The church's mission is not to change the world by using the world's tools. We have been given *spiritual* tools—the Word of God, the Holy Spirit, the body of Christ—because our battle is not "against flesh and blood, but against principalities, against powers, against the rulers of the darkness of this age" (Ephesians 6:12).

Something is terribly wrong if the world can't see the "old rugged cross" because we've surrounded it with white picket fences and American flags. Nothing should obscure the Cross. "And I, if I am lifted up from the earth," Jesus said, "will draw all peoples to Myself" (John 12:32). Paul wrote that "I determined not to know anything among you except Jesus Christ and Him crucified" (1 Corinthians 2:2). Of course, the gospel will change more than the heart. It transforms relationships, neighborhoods, and even nations. But it all starts, as Paul reminds us, with the central message of the Cross of Jesus Christ. When the world equates the message of the Cross with political and cultural values instead of spiritual truths, then the church has failed in its defining mission.

What are the consequences of this failure? A college student in Oregon who is worried about global warming may turn away from the Cross if faith in Christ (to him) means indifference to the environment. An African-American woman in downtown St. Louis may hesitate before the Cross if faith in Christ (to her) means lobbying against quotas or a raise in the minimum wage. A Muslim in suburban Detroit, though attracted to the gospel of peace, might turn away from the Cross if he believes that faith in Christ requires a blanket endorsement of American foreign policy. The point is not the rightness or wrongness of any of these positions. Christians are to be good citizens, concerned about their world and their fellow human beings. The point is, rather, that no good thing can ever substitute for the message of the Cross.

The most grievous casualty in this civil war is not the heart of a nation but the heart of the church. We compromise the vitality of our witness and our spiritual integrity as ambassadors for Christ when we identify the church with a political system of this world's making. We are called to be watchmen in the world, like the prophet Ezekiel, warning of God's certain judgment and pointing the lost to the forgiveness found only in Christ:

> When I say to the wicked, "You shall surely die," and you give him no warning, nor speak to warn the wicked from his wicked way, to save his life, that same wicked man shall die in his iniquity; but his blood I will require at your hand. EZEKIEL 3:18

With the same kind of urgency, Paul told the Corinthians to "awake to righteousness, and sin not; for some have not the knowledge of God" (1 Corinthians 15:34, KJV). We can and should have biblical positions on the moral issues of our day, but it is not through the political process that we fulfill our obligations as watchmen. We warn the world when we confront it with the blunt message of the Cross—a message of divine judgment but also of love and forgiveness. Blood will be required of us if we turn people away from that message because we have made a stumbling block with our own personal agendas. The Cross—not our politics—should be the world's stumbling block (see 1 Corinthians 1:23).

I fear we've been motivated too often by an illusion, a false assumption about our "Christian legacy." In defense of our Christian heritage and in an effort to "take back America," evangelicals have become warriors on the losing side of culture. We have nailed the Cross to ballot initiatives, slates of candidates, and political parties. Pulpits have been surrendered to politicians. Millions of voting guides have been distributed in the pews. Before the witness of an unbelieving world, we have subjected the Cross to the vagaries of public opinion and the vulgarities of raw political competition. The tragic irony is that we are on the winning side of the great spiritual battle of the cosmos, but we're on the losing side of school boards and zoning commissions, corporate marketing campaigns and Supreme Court decisions. Christ has triumphed indeed, but the world wouldn't know it by the colossal defeats we drag His reputation through.

The answer is not for the evangelical church to adopt different policies—"winning" policies shaped by focus groups, the way a political party interested only in political gamesmanship might do. The answer is not to present a more genial political face to the student in Oregon, the woman in St. Louis, or the Muslim in Detroit. The answer is to drop our political mask altogether so the world can see instead the face of Christ.

The historical and cultural evidence provides an uncertain foundation for the evangelical church. Our only option, then, is to return to our true foundation.

No other foundation can anyone lay than that which is laid, which is
Jesus Christ. 1 CORINTHIANS 3:11

Have we divided our allegiance between the Kingdom of Heaven and
the shining city on a hill? Have we been seduced by the false claims of
American exceptionalism? These are uncomfortable questions for many of
us to consider. They hit too close to home. These questions are bound up
tightly with our values, our identities, our most cherished beliefs. But Jesus
established an uncomfortable threshold for following Him—and there's
no exemption written into Scripture for American evangelicals. Like the
man who wanted first to bury his father, we must question our priorities,
examine our allegiances, and sift our motives if we want to follow Christ.

☆

Where is God's country?

From the beginning, people have always wanted God to dwell in
a hut in the middle of our own little village. Or in a beautiful temple
overlooking the city. We have always carved sacred spaces out of the
landscape as if to designate the very place where God is. Christians are
no different. Like medieval pilgrims, we still flock to what we call the
Holy Land as though there's something spiritual about the rocks and
dirt, the GPS coordinates even, where Jesus walked. But that's exactly
the false religious mind-set Jesus Himself rejected, especially when He
traveled out of His way into Samaria (definitely *not* God's country),
stopped at a well, and had a conversation with a woman about where
and how we worship God. "Our fathers worshiped on this mountain,"
the woman said to Jesus, "and you Jews say that in Jerusalem is the
place where one ought to worship." Jesus responded to the woman's
geographical limitation of God:

The hour is coming when you will neither on this mountain, nor in Jerusalem, worship the Father. . . . But the hour is coming, and now is, when the true worshipers will worship the Father in spirit and truth; for the Father is seeking such to worship Him. God is Spirit, and those who worship Him must worship in spirit and truth.

JOHN 4:21, 23-24

The great message of the Incarnation is that Jesus became flesh and dwelled among us—*all* of us. He lowered Himself from the glory of heaven, not to take ownership of the land He walked on, not to scout out real estate and plant flags, but to display the glory of His Father. Yes, a kingdom was being established; but this Kingdom, unlike all the shining cities that have come and gone, would be built in the hearts of people through repentance, obedience, and faith. In the Sermon on the Mount, Jesus challenged us to reject the glittering, empty promises of this worldly kingdom. The apostle Paul, too, constantly reminded the early church to look beyond the false promises of this world: "Set your mind on things above," Paul urged, "not on things on the earth" (Colossians 3:2).

Where is God's country?

When I was on a mission trip to Nepal, I was surprised, and saddened, to learn that some Nepali Christians, like some American evangelicals, believe that "America is where God is." When you hear that, you just want to say: *No, no, America is not where God is, even though America is a wonderful place. You can find Piggly Wigglys here, and Starbucks, and Wal-Marts. You can find freedom and opportunity, and yes, lots and lots of churches. God has blessed us and God is certainly here, but He's in Nepal and China and Argentina too. He's wherever men and women have opened their lives to His grace and opened their hearts to Christ.*

Hearts that have been redeemed. *That's* God's country.

CHAPTER THREE

Rethinking the Shining City

Together, we can once again make America the "shining city on a hill"
envisioned by the Founding Fathers.

— GARY BAUER FOR PRESIDENT 2000 CAMPAIGN BROCHURE

☆　☆　☆

The belief that America has been elected by God for a special destiny in the
world has . . . passed into the realm of motivational myths.

— KEVIN PHILLIPS

I'm going to show you where the first missionaries lived many years ago,"
Bob said as we scrambled onto the back of the pickup truck. Then he
took us, a handful of missionary kids, down a dusty, overgrown, seldom-
traveled road deep into the African bush—past villages, past stretches
of jungle, past fields of *gozo*, the starchy cassava or manioc root that was
the staple of the local diet. We stopped at a small village, one of many
we'd passed through, and Bob pointed up to a hill. "I want you to know
about the missionaries from the old days," he said. "People have forgotten them."

Most of the mission stations in Central Africa were located on high
ground, some on hills or slopes overlooking the thatched-roof huts below.
Villagers avoided the high places, since hills were one of those spots—like
springs and rivers—where the evil spirits dwelled. These were always the

best places for missionaries to settle. Hills offered some protection, and nobody disputed with them over the land.

We walked under the plentiful shade of mango trees that had been planted along the ridge by the missionaries. "Here's where they lived," Bob said. Fifty rainy seasons had taken their toll, and little remained but the foundations and a few slight mounds where sun-dried bricks had weathered to the ground. We could trace out where the houses once stood, but not much more. Still, I was fascinated by the ruins of the old mission compound that dated back to the 1920s. Even as a boy, I found myself strangely drawn to the past. These weren't the ruins of Greece or Rome, but they were ruins nonetheless.

Bob wasn't a history buff or a college professor like I turned out to be. He was a mechanic with little formal education who knew how to fix things and keep them running on the mission field. It wasn't some strange fascination with ruins that drew him to this site. He wanted us to remember that missionaries had come and gone before us. He wanted to remind us that others had made great sacrifices and laid a foundation for the work we were carrying on. Bob seemed to think a lot about this. Once he overheard me making some lighthearted reference to a grave on the compound where we lived—the grave of an American missionary whose name I didn't even know, someone who had died in the 1940s and was buried in the African soil—and he rebuked me sharply. I deserved it. What did I know of the sacrifices those pioneers had made? I should have known better, since I'd seen the sacrifices of my own parents.

The first missionaries, like settlers on the American frontier, were a tough and hardy lot. They knew how to keep machines running when there weren't any more spare parts. They rigged up our mission station with old World War II–era military phones—the kind you cranked by hand. (Two long rings and one short was our number.) When fuel pumps conked out on some remote road, they learned how to prop up a jerrican under the hood, strap it down with rubber, and create a gravity flow of gasoline just sufficient to get them back to the mission station. We had printers and plumbers, electricians and mechanics, nurses and pharmacists, teachers and truck drivers in our little communities scattered on the hills of Central Africa. These were ordinary men and women who felt God's call in their lives to go to this most remote place on the African continent.

They weren't always successful in separating the Western culture they brought with them from the irreducible message of the gospel. Missionary methods betrayed a deep cultural ignorance and bias. Native pastors were taught to wear white shirts and dark ties in the pulpit. American hymns by Fanny Crosby were wrenched into the Sango dialect and then set to the same melodies we sang back home, which, given the pentatonic musical traditions of sub-Saharan Africa, was like forcing square pegs into round holes. Despite the missionaries' best efforts, Fanny Crosby always ended up sounding like the blues. There was legalism and hypocrisy on the mission field too. Missionaries bickered and gossiped. And there was politics, always politics.

But somehow, God still worked—as He always does.

In the intervening years, I've thought a lot about what we build on hills and what comes of those projects. I've thought about the faithfulness of men and women who maybe didn't know enough about culture—either their own culture back in America or the one they came to evangelize. But they knew one big thing about God: that He loves us, sent His Son to save us, and commissioned us to share the Good News with others. Not much was left of those brick houses on the hill in Central Africa. The little compound under a mango grove had come to nothing. But the work of Christ continues. The old rhyme captures the great truth: "Only one life, 'twill soon be past; only what's done for Christ will last." What kind of city are we building on the hill? Who is doing the building? And what kind of people are we becoming in the process? The missionaries I knew as a child didn't always succeed in disentangling their cultural values from the gospel. But despite their blind spots, cultural deficiencies, and human weaknesses, they understood that the gospel, and only the gospel, is the power of God unto salvation (see Romans 1:16). What about us? Have we lost sight of this great calling and become instead partisan defenders of a culture, its values, and its myths?

Just as Christians in the Roman Empire had to disentangle their faith from the cultural values of the world around them, so also we as American evangelicals must clearly understand the origin and authority of our beliefs. Evangelicals have adopted the language and values of our culture, allowing the myths of culture—not the truths of Scripture—to shape how we interact with the world, how we view our national history, and how we articulate our core values. This is the second false assumption that motivates evangelical activism in the political sphere. We've casually accepted the secular doctrine that America is a shining city on a hill, populated by a tenaciously self-reliant and practical people. We have Christianized these humanistic values—myths of utopia, self-reliance, and pragmatism—and have compromised the message and ministry of the church. But nothing can be assumed as a cultural birthright, immune from the judgments of Scripture. Every thought, every myth, must be taken captive to Christ.

UTOPIA

From the writings of John Winthrop in the seventeenth century through the speeches of Ronald Reagan, the vision of America as a utopian experiment—"the last best hope for mankind"—has held a powerful sway over our imagination. The dream of a perfect society, a utopia, is not an American creation, of course, but a persistent theme in the political theories of the Western world. As far back as the ancient Greeks, Plato presented his vision of a philosophical utopia in his greatest work, *The Republic*. During the Age of Discovery, too, new worlds were imagined even as new worlds were explored. Men like Columbus thought they might even find heaven on earth if they just kept looking. In 1516, the English humanist Sir Thomas More drafted his own version of a perfect society and coined the word we still use, *utopia*, to describe it. (Significantly, utopia means "no place.") With material progress came new possibilities for human perfection, including the "worker's paradise" of Karl Marx's *Communist Manifesto* (1848) and the social engineering of the modern welfare state. Aware in our souls that we were expelled from paradise, humankind has been trying ever since to recreate its own.

The American utopia crystallized in our imagination in the nineteenth century and was an effective counterbalance to the various socialist myths of Europe. Karl Marx and Friedrich Engels speculated long and hard in their correspondence as to why socialism was not taking root in America. Part of the answer lay in our mythology; the American Dream did just fine in answering these basic human desires for progress and a betterment of the human condition. We have our own utopia, and it's bolder than all the European prototypes. We actually locate our utopia in time and space. We point to it and dare to say, "From sea to shining sea—*this is it.*"

Not surprisingly, the American utopian myth was always framed in both metaphysical and material terms. All the way back in 1630, the myth was given its classic American form by John Winthrop, who was both a devout Puritan and the head of a trading company. Before the colonists sailed from England in the *Arbella* to found the Massachusetts Bay

Colony, Winthrop preached a sermon, "A Model of Christian Charity," that included these famous words:

> We must consider that we shall be as a city upon a hill. The eyes of all people are upon us. So that if we shall deal falsely with our God in this work we have undertaken . . . we shall be made a story and a by-word through the world. We shall open the mouths of enemies to speak evil of the ways of God. . . . We shall shame the faces of many of God's worthy servants, and cause their prayers to be turned into curses upon us till we be consumed out of the good land whither we are going.

The history of America is a history of contradictions, and Winthrop's speech reminds us how far back these contradictions run. The image of the city on a hill is taken from the Sermon on the Mount (see Matthew 5:14), but Winthrop's language and ideas clearly invoke the Old Testament and God's dealings with Israel. Winthrop believed that England stood in a covenant relationship with God but that England had violated that covenant. It was therefore up to Puritans like Winthrop and the Pilgrims he led to fulfill a new covenant with God in the New World. The young colony would be like Israel among the nations, showing to old Europe what a true Christian community should look like. Since life in a city is impossible without order, structure, limits, and restrictions, the Puritan city—like ancient Israel—would be governed by a rigid understanding of God's law. Like Israel, this city would be a community of believers, defined by its collective obedience to God and holding little regard for individual rights of belief and self-expression. John Winthrop's city was never intended to be a pluralistic melting pot of cultures and values. Nor did it reflect in any way the Kingdom teaching of the Sermon on the Mount.

The exceptional status of America as a new Israel is a common theme in our national life. During the American Revolution, for example, the image of the young nation as a New Israel, shaking off slavery in Egypt and embracing freedom in Canaan, recurred in the political and religious rhetoric of the day. In a sermon preached in Concord, New Hampshire, in 1788, Samuel Langdon looked back a few years to remember how "God hath graciously patronized our cause and taken us under his special care, as he did his ancient covenant people." Benjamin Franklin and Thomas Jefferson, among the least religious of our Founding Fathers, both agreed in 1776 that "Promised Land" imagery should adorn the nation's seal. Jefferson would return again to this theme later, as in his second inaugural address (1805): "I shall need ... the favor of that Being in whose hands we are, who led our fathers, as Israel of old, from their native land and planted them in a country flowing with all the necessities and comforts of life." The theme was developed further by some of our greatest writers in the nineteenth century, among them Herman Melville, who freely mixes up the language of 1 Peter 2:9 with the imagery of the Old Testament and the American frontier:

> We Americans are the peculiar, chosen people—the Israel of our time; we bear the ark of the liberties of the world. God has predestined, mankind expects, great things from our race; and great things we feel in our souls. The rest of the nations must soon be in our rear. We are pioneers of the world; the advance-guard, sent on through the wilderness of untried things, to break a new path in the New World that is ours.

It's curious, though, how this confidence in God's divine mandate is expressed alongside a powerful national hubris: "We are pioneers of the world," Melville declared. We will "break a new path in the New World that is ours." Melville continues in a vein that becomes increasingly idolatrous:

Long enough have we been skeptics with regard to ourselves, and doubted whether, indeed, the political Messiah had come. But he has come in *us*, if we would but give utterance to his promptings. And let us always remember that with ourselves, almost for the first time in the history of earth, national selfishness is unbounded philanthropy; for we can not do a good to America but we give alms to the world.

Melville was a great writer, but he was no theologian. This may be the most troubling paraphrase of American exceptionalism ever offered. Our interest becomes the world's interest, whether the world realizes it or not, because we have a divine mandate backing up our actions. Like Winthrop's city, Melville's America is a beacon to the world. "God has given to us, for a future inheritance," Melville claimed, "the broad domains of the political pagans, that shall yet come and lie down under the shade of the ark, without bloody hands being lifted." America had become the millennial kingdom.

But Melville was wrong. Bloody hands *were* lifted against the native populations of North America as the New Israel took possession of Canaan. The logic of this was inevitable. If America was the Promised Land and the settlers were Israel, then the native populations were pagan Canaanites who had to be subdued or destroyed. And bloody hands were lifted in slave markets, too. Millions of Africans were transported to the New World not to "lie down under the shade of the ark" but to work in cotton fields under the scorching sun.

Of course, Jesus intended none of this when He spoke of a city on a hill. He was not picturing a New Israel. He was addressing His Kingdom ethic to individuals, not nations. The myth of American exceptionalism rests upon a mishandling of Scripture that is grotesque in scale and terrible in its consequences. Believers have no need to pursue an exceptional political kingdom when we have an exceptional Savior. Still, the idea that America is a New Israel, elected out of the nations by God, persists in the rhetoric of the Religious Right. The frequent invocation of 2 Chronicles 7:14 (KJV) is a case in point.

> If my people, which are called by my name, shall humble themselves, and pray, and seek my face, and turn from their wicked ways; then will I hear from heaven, and will forgive their sin, and will heal their land.

This call to repentance was specifically cited by the organizers of the April 28, 1980, Washington for Jesus rally—one of the first big political rallies staged by the Religious Right. One cannot address this passage to the American people without already assuming that America is "God's people, called by God's name." If this message, which was addressed to Solomon and the nation of Israel, has any relevance to us today (which it certainly does), then its relevance must be felt by the church, the body of Christ, and by individual believers. The church, not America, needs to humble itself. The church, not America, needs to pray and seek God's face. The church, not America, needs to turn from its wicked ways. And this is because the church—not America—is God's people, called by God's name. Religious conservatives today, like John Winthrop centuries ago, make a profound mistake when they interpret Scripture through the filter of a cultural myth.

☆

This Puritan vision of a city on a hill would not survive the westward expansion of America. Winthrop had imagined his little settlement as an eastward-looking city, a vibrant witness to an apostate Europe. Melville retained something of this eastward perspective as he pictured the entire world watching us, expecting "great things from our race." But Melville's perspective, like America's, was also shifting westward. "The rest of the nations must soon be in our rear," Melville boasted. "We are pioneers of the world; the advance-guard, sent on through the wilderness of untried things, to break a new path in the New World that is ours." As America matured in the nineteenth century, pushing ever deeper into the frontier, our utopian vision shifted west as well. The city became a garden of freedom and opportunity. The limits of the city were traded in for the limitless spaces of the "Garden of the World," as the Western frontier was called. Moral rectitude was cashed in for material prosperity. This garden was nothing less than a restored Garden of Eden, an earthly paradise that humankind has been searching to reclaim ever since the Fall. Ultimately, it would take Ronald Reagan to revive the old Puritan metaphor and bring city and garden together. In so doing, Reagan would author a great political success story, but he would also leave us with a remarkable package of contradictions.

The odd mixture of theology and material power—the notion that you can do God's work while building your own kingdom—predates John Winthrop, Herman Melville, and Ronald Reagan. We find it all the way back in the letters Columbus sent home to the king and queen of Spain. Adventurers in the fifteenth and sixteenth centuries imagined that they were close to finding the original Garden of Eden. Columbus in particular was consumed by the search for "Paradise Lost," as his notebooks, annotations, and letters reveal. After discovering Hispaniola in the Caribbean, Columbus sent voluminous notes back to the Spanish monarchs, describing the beauty of the islands, the abundance of food, and the innocence of the natives. Eden couldn't be far away, he reasoned. "We can convert these gentle people," Columbus argued, "and then put them to work for Spain." And who would receive the glory? The king and queen of Spain, of course.

> Since our Redeemer has given the victory to our most illustrious
> King and Queen, and to their renowned kingdoms, in so great a
> matter, for this all Christendom ought to feel delight and make
> great feasts and give solemn thanks to the Holy Trinity, with
> many solemn prayers for the great exaltation which they shall
> have in the turning of so many peoples to our holy faith, and
> afterwards for the temporal benefits, because not only Spain but
> all Christendom will have hence refreshment and gain.

Here are the abiding contradictions of American history—already in place before America was even an idea. All the "temporal benefits" and "refreshment and gain" of material prosperity could be achieved in the service of God. In the end, America would not be Spanish, nor would it be Catholic, but it would certainly become the compromised utopia that Columbus had imagined.

A century later, the English explorations of Virginia under Queen Elizabeth I did much to promote the view that the New World was a garden paradise. While some exuded about the natural beauty and fertility of the land (Arthur Barlow wrote in 1584 that "the earth bringeth forth all things in abundance as in the first creation, without toil or labor"), others were more materialistic, less "biblical" in their language. Thomas Hariot's report to Raleigh (1585) is subdivided into three chapters: "Merchantable commodities," "Commodities for sustenance of man's life," and "Commodities for building and other necessary uses." These were the first awestruck impressions that Europeans had, and would continue to have, of America. The sense of wonder at the bounty, beauty, and almost unlimited potential of the American continent would only increase as settlers pushed into the heartland. Eden was also open for business, a rich garden of "merchantable commodities" to be exploited for material gain. This joining of theology and economics would become one of the central ironies of American conservatism. A cartoon in the *New Yorker* nails the contradiction with characteristic wit. One pilgrim on the *Mayflower* turns to another and says, "Religious freedom is my immediate goal, but my long-range plan is to go into real estate."

As settlers poured into the fertile plains and rich valleys of the Western frontier, they did, in fact, "go into real estate." Along the way, they managed to slough off the moralizing strictures of Puritan New England. The West was a land of freedom and opportunity. For some it would even be a land of escape and new identity. People could reinvent themselves in a land this big. Land was cheap. Laws were few and far between. The young nation expanded into the wide-open spaces of the American continent, and in turn, the continent expanded our vision of ourselves. The moral heart of American conservatism may belong to the Puritan city, but its material soul, with its love of political and economic freedom, was cultivated in the garden of the West.

Three hundred and fifty years after Winthrop preached his sermon, a "cowboy" rode out of the West toward Washington. Ronald Reagan followed his remarkable intuition. He knew in his gut that America was both moral and material, both a city and a garden. Reagan refurbished the city on a hill—it was now a "shining city"—and he reintroduced it to the American people in his presidential campaign. This city had been a fixture of Reagan's political vocabulary for years, but in 1980 the metaphor found its time—as destiny would have it. I remember the speech he gave on Labor Day that year, which used to be the traditional kickoff date for presidential campaigns. As I watched the news coverage, I was mesmerized by the symbolism, by the astonishing combination of icons and myths. There he stood on the New York harbor with the Statue of Liberty and Ellis Island as a backdrop. His normally immovable hair was tossing gently in the wind as he presented his vision of an America that renewed its promise with the past and looked to the future with unflinching optimism.

Eight years later Reagan invoked the imagery one last time in the farewell address he delivered from the Oval Office. "I've spoken of the shining city all my political life," he said, "but I don't know if I ever quite communicated what I saw when I said it." What Reagan went on to describe was a potent combination of Winthrop's moral city and the material garden of the Western frontier.

In my mind it was a tall, proud city built on rocks stronger than oceans, windswept, God-blessed, and teeming with people of all kinds living in harmony and peace, a city with free ports that hummed with commerce and creativity, and if there had to be city walls, the walls had doors and the doors were open to anyone with the will and the heart to get here. That's how I saw it and see it still.

There are contradictions here, of course, but these are the contradictions that make up America. Reagan pictures a nation that is God-fearing but also humanistic and self-sufficient. His city looks eastward as a beacon of hope toward Europe, but it also looks westward to the land of opportunity. It is a moral, "God-blessed" city, but (with low taxes and reduced federal regulation) it is also humming "with commerce and creativity."

Reagan had no choice but to transform Winthrop's city—shine it up, so to speak—since Winthrop's moral utopia was actually closer to European prototypes than to the Western garden. Winthrop's community was structured and orderly, much as Plato's republic, More's utopia, and Marx's worker's paradise. The Mayflower Compact, drafted in 1620 as the first governing document in Plymouth, Massachusetts, has traditionally been taught to schoolchildren as a charter of liberty, even though its main preoccupation (and rightly so) was with order and social stability. There was very little "democracy" in either the Mayflower Compact or Winthrop's sermon "A Model of Christian Charity." Winthrop's conception of social structure is utterly medieval in its hierarchical ordering: "God Almighty in His most holy and wise providence, hath so disposed of the condition of mankind, as in all times some must be rich, some poor, some high and eminent in power and dignity, others mean and in subjection." But unlike Winthrop's city of collective uniformity, Reagan's city—like the Western frontier itself—is "teeming with people of all kinds." Reagan's city is a heaven on earth for those who have "the will and the heart" to get there by their own efforts. God's role, it would appear, has been reduced to smiling down benevolently on all His children who are living in "harmony and peace."

Reagan's critics always underestimated him. They never fully grasped the breadth of what he managed to accomplish by weaving together two entirely different visions of America:

Puritan myth	frontier myth
"city"	"garden"
moral utopia	materialistic utopia
Eastward looking	Westward looking
religious	secular
defined by limits	defined by freedom
ordered space	open space
collective	individualistic

Reagan spoke a mythological language that evangelicals understood well, even if we had to disregard a whole lot of false theology along the way. But in the end, Reagan was never one of us. Not really. Not in his fundamental understanding of the nature of God and humanity. Reagan drew from the deep taproot of American mythology, not biblical truth.

We adopted him as our spokesman, but we never questioned the utopian mingling of political, economic, social, and religious themes. Reagan had fused the city and garden together into a paradoxical vision of America—one of the most remarkable achievements in the long history of American political rhetoric. It was a glorious if unsustainable myth, and we were unwilling to see the contradictions.

A great contradiction does lie at the heart of the American personality. The New World was discovered by monarchs and trading companies who were pursuing power and wealth, but it was settled (in part) by deeply religious men and women who believed passionately in the transcendent values of revealed religion. This contradiction has never been resolved, which is why our history gives us so many conflicting messages. For most of our history, though, these competing sets of values were held in a delicate balance. The religious imagery coexisted (and sometimes even legitimized) the humanistic and materialistic themes of expansion, growth, individual freedom, and opportunity. Reagan would give us the last great synthesis of these contradictory instincts. What was once a set of paradoxes in our national psyche has today become an open civil war of values. The imagery and phraseology of religion, allowed to exist within a largely humanistic framework of ideas, are now being purged through legal challenges and broader cultural shifts. The stridency of the debate between Left and Right, and the hostility and outright contempt that secular elites display toward religious conservatives, testify to the fact that we're now entering the end of a long process. We're becoming the post-Christian nation we were always destined to be.

The question for evangelicals in the twenty-first century is this: Can we see these contradictions now? Can we see the idol we have made out of America? Over a hundred years ago, a Hungarian scholar confronted us with this very question. Born in Hungary in 1854, Dr. Emil Reich was educated in Prague, Budapest, and Vienna before emigrating with his family to America in 1884. Ultimately, in 1893 he settled in London, where he became a popular lecturer and commentator on history and society. His observations about American nationalism are as true today as they were at the end of the nineteenth century.

> The Americans are filled with such an implicit and absolute confidence in their Union and in their future success that any remark other than laudatory is unacceptable to the majority of them. We have had many opportunities of hearing public speakers in America cast doubts upon the very existence of God and of Providence, question the historic nature or veracity of the whole fabric of Christianity; but never has it been our fortune to catch the slightest whisper of doubt, the slightest want of faith, in the chief God of America—unlimited belief in the future of America.

Of course, America has many detractors today, the so-called "blame America first" brand of American liberalism. But Reich's words still ring true for conservatives. Indeed, Reagan's city has become an idol to many evangelical Christians. A generation after Reagan swept into the White House, religious conservatives are searching for new national leaders to carry their message and promote their values. They are looking for a new "political messiah," someone who is "Reaganesque." Someone who embodies the utopian spirit of American nationalism, who holds "unlimited belief in the future of America." Patriotism can be a good and natural thing, but idolatry is always wrong.

We can—in fact, we *must*—learn something from the early church, especially as our own national experience reflects so closely the materialism and idolatry of the ancient world. The Roman Empire had its own "shining city on a hill," or *seven* hills to be exact, founded by exiles from an old country. The poet Virgil told the legend of how Aeneas sailed from Troy with a small band of refugees after the city was overrun by the Greeks. Rome is thus connected with the "old world" of ancient Troy and Greece but is also forward looking, westward looking. The Roman gods looked favorably upon this desolate little band, and they became a people of destiny. Rome was to become the Eternal City, the defender of civilized values, the last best hope for mankind.

The Roman Empire was at the height of its power when Jesus delivered the Sermon on the Mount. Roman propagandists were busy peddling their nationalistic myth of destiny and material progress—all of which was embodied in the Eternal City built on seven hills. But none of this impressed Jesus. His city would be built in the hearts of people. His city would not be built by Trojan refugees or representatives of the Massachusetts Trading Company or religious conservatives electing the "right people" to Congress. His city would be built by the progress of the gospel.

What does Jesus have to offer in place of the worldly utopias of Rome, Marx, and America? Sacrifice and self-denial. Jesus disappointed many of His followers when He preached that the Kingdom of God would be established in the hearts of people through repentance. "We were hoping," said Cleopas on the road to Emmaus, "that it was He who was going to redeem Israel" (Luke 24:21)—the One, that is, who would throw off the yoke of Roman bondage. But even when throngs were cheering Him in the streets, Jesus refused to improvise a political solution for the world's problems. He refused the temptation of a political career and opted instead for the lonely task of doing His Father's will, even when that meant dying on a cross. Jesus asked His Father to remove the cup from Him, but there was no other way for God's work to be done. There was no political solution for the problem of our sin.

Nor did Jesus turn to the world's resources once the Cross was behind

Him. When commissioning the Twelve to go out and "make disciples of all nations," Jesus armed them not with swords but with the power of the Holy Spirit. History bears witness to the remarkable fact that Christianity grew and spread not by force of arms (as Islam did) but by believers who lived like cities on a hill in the neighborhoods and alleyways of the Roman Empire. Christ entrusted the gospel to us and empowered us with His Spirit. That's all He gave us, which means that we, like the early Christians, will just have to make do.

These early Christians were bombarded by propaganda about the Eternal City of Rome, but it didn't sway them—at least not before the time of Constantine in the early fourth century. They didn't compromise their belief that salvation belongs to the Lord, not to the legions of Rome. After Constantine's vision of a flaming cross ("By this sign you will conquer"), things changed, of course. The mission of the church was compromised. But before Constantine started conquering people in Christ's name, the early Christians had lived quiet lives marked by faith and obedience to God. They were good citizens, which is a point made repeatedly in the writings of the church fathers, but they never forgot that "our citizenship is in heaven, from which we also eagerly wait for the Savior, the Lord Jesus Christ" (Philippians 3:20). Christians of every age are to exchange the contradictions of our national myths for the clarity we find in Jesus Christ. Either we can embrace a false mythology that is ultimately destructive to the cause of the gospel or we can reawaken ourselves to the great commission that Christ gave to no nation but to the church—a divine mandate to make disciples of all nations and all peoples.

SELF-RELIANCE
From the maxims of Ben Franklin to the celebrity status of entrepreneurs like Donald Trump, the spirit of self-reliance runs deep in our historical

veins. Our heroes are cowboys and capitalists, self-made individuals who shaped the nation's destiny by the sweat of their brows. We can thank Old World Calvinism in part for this second great theme of America. The Puritans brought the Protestant work ethic with them, an ethic that emphasizes thrift, hard work, and self-denial. Beyond the theology, though, lies the commonsense reality that only tough and self-reliant people survive on the frontier and prosper. The deer and the antelope might have played on the range, but settlers worked hard from morning to night to store enough food to make it through the winter. Teddy Roosevelt described this "spirit of defiant self-reliance" in his four-volume profile of the American settler, *The Winning of the West* (1889–1896):

> Our frontiers were pushed westward by the warlike skills and adventurous personal prowess of the individual settlers. . . . Colonists fresh from the old world, no matter how thrifty, steady-going, and industrious, could not hold their own on the frontier; they had to settle where they were protected from the Indians by a living barrier of bold and self-reliant American borderers. The west would never have been settled save for the fierce courage and the eager desire to brave danger so characteristic of the stalwart backwoodsmen.

Why is self-reliance a myth? Not because it isn't true, of course, but because it *is* true at a deep level of cultural meaning. Roosevelt, himself a paragon of the self-reliant man, extols the virtues of these "grim, stern people" who were "strong and simple" and who had "the love of freedom rooted in their very hearts' core." Roosevelt's words are mythic not only because they *describe* who we are (or think we are) but also because they *prescribe* how we should live in the world.

The virtue of self-reliance is celebrated in the classic works of our national literature. The grim, stern figure of Captain Ahab in *Moby-Dick*, no less than a settler on the frontier, embodies the spirit of independence. Ahab shows us the tragic vision of American individualism—an obsessive self-assertion in the face of God and the universe. For the happy ending to the story, we can turn to the dime novels that Horatio Alger wrote in the late nineteenth century. The core myth of the American Dream is personified in the hardworking lad who pulls himself up by his bootstraps, relying on his own effort and good character to get ahead. This plotline still appeals to us, both in fiction and in real life, even if the white boy is transformed into a black woman named Oprah Winfrey who builds an empire out of her hard work and strong character.

Self-reliance has always been the surest route to creating an American success story out of one's life. The methods of achieving this success, however, have changed over time. In Ben Franklin's New England, the Puritan ethic was still sufficiently strong for personal success to be understood as the fruit of piety and economic frugality. In Horatio Alger's world, however, the emphasis had shifted to the kind of good character traits that we now associate with the entrepreneurial spirit: foresight, initiative, sound judgment, hard work, and stick-to-it-iveness. Fictional characters embodied this, but so did real people like Andrew Carnegie, who captured the American imagination in the Gilded Age of the late nineteenth century. With a new century came a new ethic of personal success: selling oneself.

The experience of the Great Depression demonstrated the central fallacy in the Horatio Alger story line: Hard work and good character are not always enough to get ahead. In 1937 Dale Carnegie, a distant cousin of the famous steel magnate, published his famously successful book, *How to Win Friends and Influence People*. Carnegie's book, which is still in print, set the standard for the self-help genre in American publishing for decades to come. In the early 1950s, a Protestant minister named Norman Vincent Peale sold millions of Americans on *The Power of Positive Thinking*. With the ability to think positively and influence people, all that Americans needed now was a good opportunity. Tupperware, Stanley Home Products, and Amway were ready to sign people up. The entrepreneurial spirit in American life continues to be—in the digital age of eBay—the main expressive outlet for American self-reliance.

An essential plank of conservative thought is that men and women should be liberated from the shackles of government control to pursue their dreams, work hard, play by the rules, and get ahead. Ronald Reagan chiseled out his political image from the raw material of this myth. He started out as the ordinary aw-shucks kid from the Midwest who made good. Bill Clinton, too, understood the power of the myth and transformed himself into the unlikely "man from Hope." A folk theology lies behind this character type, the belief that "God helps those who help themselves." It's a very old proverb, attested in many cultures and languages and quoted in Benjamin Franklin's 1736 edition of *Poor Richard's Almanack*. Though not of American origin, the proverb does seem to have found a new lease on life in the New World. It expresses the distinctly American concept of self-reliance—especially the notion that human effort is not inconsistent with divine sovereignty and grace.

Long after the last homesteader put down roots on the plains, long after the last railroad spikes were struck, we continue to celebrate the virtues of independence and rugged individualism. At its best, self-reliance builds strong people and strong nations. At its worst, it intoxicates us with a false grandeur: We are the captains of our souls. In his essay "Self-Reliance," Ralph Waldo Emerson wrote that "nothing can bring you peace but yourself." This is old-fashioned Roman Stoicism with an American twist. You can't control fate, the Stoics taught; you can't control what others do to you. But you *can* control yourself. You can govern the universe of your heart and achieve a kind of peace within a turbulent world. Stoicism was an attractive self-help philosophy in the Roman world, as it was for the gentlemen farmers in colonial Virginia who would sit on their porches reading Cicero while the slaves worked. It's still a popular philosophy of life, judging by the constant spate of self-help books that top the best-seller lists. Each one promises to deliver the secret to a better, more productive life, a better you, when you "take charge" and "make things happen." It's not so much a philosophy any longer as a cliché.

So, what's wrong with self-reliance? As parents, we want our children to grow up with self-confident and independent spirits, able to care for themselves and ready to achieve material success in the world. As citizens, we want to live in vibrant communities where people provide for their own families and refuse to become wards of the state. But the American myth of self-reliance takes us much farther than these reasonable and laudable goals. American independence is one of the most subtle expressions of human pride—subtle because it dresses itself up in so many positive attributes. The more we can rely on ourselves, the less we feel our need for God and other people. Self-reliance thus distorts our vertical relationship with God and our horizontal relationship with those around us.

Self-reliance comes with a high theological cost. We have Christianized a humanistic American value and cheapened the grace of God. Evangelicals are not free from the seduction of self-sufficiency. Christian bookstores are filled with workbooks and study guides and programs designed to help you lose weight, make more money, or just feel better about yourself. How can we testify effectively to humanity's complete need for our Creator if we don't believe it ourselves? How can we convince men and women in a post-Christian America that God is still central to the human condition if we don't live as though it's true?

The seductiveness of self-reliance is summed up by the title of a recent best seller, *Your Best Life Now: 7 Steps to Living at Your Full Potential* (2004). A troubling shift in focus away from God is evident in the first word of the title: *Your.* God has become little more than a touchstone, a reference point for how *you* can have a happy and successful Christian life. The title is the first clue that something is terribly wrong with this new pragmatic brand of Christianity. As we open the book and work through the seven steps, we soon realize that we've entered a material world where the Holy Spirit has taken a backseat to the ghost of Norman Vincent Peale.

We are encouraged, for instance, to "enlarge your vision" of our own potential. But the prophet Isaiah has told us instead to enlarge our vision of God's holiness (see Isaiah 6). Our vision of who we are actually gets much smaller when we see God in all His glory. Saul of Tarsus had a highly developed sense of his own potential long before he met Christ on the road to Damascus, as he reminded us in Philippians 3:4-10:

> If anyone else thinks he may have confidence in the flesh, I more
> so: circumcised the eighth day, of the stock of Israel, of the tribe of
> Benjamin, a Hebrew of the Hebrews; concerning the law, a Pharisee;
> concerning zeal, persecuting the church; concerning the righteous-
> ness which is in the law, blameless.

Saul's self-reliant heart was broken when Christ confronted him with the glory of God. Saul's world, with all its values and achievements, suddenly turned upside down.

> But what things were gain to me, these I have counted loss for Christ.
> Yet indeed I also count all things loss for the excellence of the knowl-

edge of Christ Jesus my Lord, for whom I have suffered the loss of all things, and count them as rubbish, that I may gain Christ and be found in Him, not having my own righteousness, which is from the law, but that which is through faith in Christ, the righteousness which is from God by faith; that I may know Him and the power of His resurrection, and the fellowship of His sufferings, being conformed to His death.

Knowing Christ was the only thing that really mattered to Paul. The material things of this world were so diminished in value that they became like common trash to him. My guess is that the word *you* in a title will sell more books than the word *trash* ever will. But then Paul wasn't selling books. He was showing us how we can know God—how we can *really* know Him—by dying to ourselves and all the rubbish of this world.

We're also advised to "develop a healthy self-image." But Paul has given us the right example by telling us that he was the least of the apostles, one "not worthy" of the calling God placed on his life. Paul reminded us that we already think of ourselves "more highly than [we] ought to think" (Romans 12:3). Instead, we need to think of ourselves the way God does. We need the humility of John the Baptist, who understood that he must "decrease" if Christ was to "increase" and be magnified (John 3:30). We need to tremble before our Creator the way Peter did when he declared to Jesus, "Depart from me, for I am a sinful man" (Luke 5:8). We need to see ourselves the way Nebuchadnezzar did after God humbled him. Here was another man who had no problems with self-esteem—a poster boy for self-reliance as he marveled at the works of his own hands.

At the end of the twelve months [Nebuchadnezzar] was walking about the royal palace of Babylon. The king spoke, saying, "Is not this great Babylon, that I have built for a royal dwelling by my mighty power and for the honor of my majesty?" DANIEL 4:29-30

God's lesson in self-reliance was swift and decisive. Nebuchadnezzar was driven from the palace to live like a wild man among the beasts of the field. Only when he acknowledged the sovereignty of God over all things, including his little kingdom, did Nebuchadnezzar's sense return to him.

The best-selling book also counsels us to "discover the power" of our thoughts and words. David, however, reminds us to revel in the transforming power of God's Word by meditating on it day and night (see Psalm 1:2). The book has sold thousands of copies, but it's only telling us what we want to hear. Our ears are itching for this humanistic message, because our culture has programmed us to accept these dangerous clichés as if they were self-evident truths. But as *World* magazine editor Gene Veith has reminded us, Christianity flourishes "not by trying to offer people what they already have, but by offering them what they desperately lack—namely, the Word of God and salvation through Jesus Christ."

Satan loves self-reliance, as it directly undermines our dependence on God. A self-reliant person may see the need for God only in a foxhole or in a hospital waiting room. David reminded us that we need God in every circumstance of our lives: "Trust in Him *at all times*, you people" (Psalm 62:8, emphasis added). Our uncritical and unreflective embrace of self-reliance—under the guise of "positive thinking" and "healthy self-esteem"—blinds us to our spiritual need and nullifies the gospel. Satan tried to keep Jesus from the Cross. Failing that, he now tries to steer you and me away from the clear message of human weakness conquered by divine grace.

Paul understood that self-reliance and self-denial are incompatible values. He was schooled in the Hellenistic philosophies of his day, and we hear echoes of Stoic philosophy in this autobiographical passage:

> Not that I speak in regard to need, for I have learned in whatever state I am, to be content: I know how to be abased, and I know how to abound. Everywhere and in all things I have learned both to be full and to be hungry, both to abound and to suffer need. I can do all things through Christ who strengthens me. **PHILIPPIANS 4:11-13**

A Roman Stoic could have agreed with Paul—right up to that last sentence. Stoicism, which was the dominant self-help philosophy of the Roman world, taught that we cannot control anything but our own hearts. We cannot control fate. We cannot control circumstances. We cannot control how others treat us. But we *can* control our responses and emotions. The Stoic would say, "I can do all things through *myself.*" Paul replied, "I can do all things through *Christ.*"

Jesus taught us to pray, "Give us this day our daily bread" as a necessary reminder that we depend on His grace not just for the really big things like salvation but for the most basic things in our lives as well. Our daily bread may come from the beak of a raven, as it did for the prophet Elijah in the wilderness. It may come in the form of a mass-produced bag of white Wonder Bread, stacked in the grocery store as the end product of American ingenuity and efficiency. But ultimately, our daily bread comes from the hand of God.

Self-reliance does more than distort our vertical relationship with God. It also distorts our horizontal relationships within society and leads to two specific deficits: our sense of community and our degree of compassion. Christians can often be "community-challenged" individuals who forget that God did not create us to be lone rangers but individuals who function within social networks of family, friends, communities, and nations. We should not cede to anyone the concept of community in either the political or spiritual arena. God has ordained civil government, and Christians should lead the way in modeling what "civil" discourse should be in a pluralistic community. God has also placed Christians in the body of Christ, and we are to function as a community of believers—not as a loosely confederated band of religious freelancers and entrepreneurs.

Compassion, too, should be a distinguishing feature of the church. But when Christians explicitly align themselves with a political philosophy widely caricatured (even if wrongly so) as heartlessly individualistic, then we misrepresent the cause of Christ to the world. The fact that George W. Bush packaged himself as a *compassionate* conservative in his 2000 presidential run confirms the popular view of conservatism as a sink-or-swim and dog-eat-dog view of life. Christians should never have to ask the world to take a second look at us and see that we're really compassionate Christians, after all. Whatever else the world may think of us, they should hear the love of Christ in our words and see it demonstrated in the way we treat others.

PRACTICALITY

More than any other nation in history, America was founded on a great idea—the power of freedom to unleash the potential in the human spirit. This has been our greatest contribution to the world's bank of ideas, but it's been articulated most clearly in the practical outworkings of national experience, not in philosophical treatises. Thomas Jefferson might have captured this idea in the beautiful opening paragraph of the Declaration of Independence and Lincoln might have restated it with grandeur in the Gettysburg Address, but the main monuments that testify to this idea are the settlements, frontiers, railroads, factories, and battlefields of our national history. And it had to be this way. America was an invention, something to be built from the ground up. America might have been inspired by a great idea, but this idea would be worthless if never hewn out of the forests of a continent. Our most creative minds—people like Benjamin Franklin, Henry Ford, and Bill Gates—have influenced the world by what they *did*, not by what they *thought*.

We are a practical-minded people who are naturally suspicious of intellectuals. And though we're impatient with critical inquiry, we have always been a clever people looking to improve every mousetrap. The can-do philosophy of NASA runs deep in our national veins. Our heroes are frontiersmen like Daniel Boone, tinkerers like Thomas Edison, and explorers like Lewis and Clark. The iconic figures of our culture are portrayed in the movies by strong-jawed men who speak little but act quickly—John Wayne, Gary Cooper, and Clint Eastwood. Given the choice between an inarticulate man of action and an egghead with a silver tongue (which pretty much describes the 1952 and 1956 face-offs between Dwight Eisenhower and Adlai Stevenson), the American people will choose the man of action every time. In the 1992 presidential campaign, Ross Perot surprised political pundits with his broad appeal to the American people. Washington insiders might have viewed Perot as a quirky little man who was slightly paranoid. Millions of Americans, however, responded to his mythic combination of self-reliance and homespun practicality. "It's time to get under the hood," he would say in his Texas twang, "and fix the problem."

The first settlers had neither the time nor the inclination to set up philosophical reading clubs when they landed in Jamestown four hundred years ago. Walls had to be built around the camp and food had to be gathered and stockpiled if they were to survive the first long winter in 1607. Survival in a new land imposed a harsh set of priorities that our nation has never forgotten. Those who pushed the American idea ever deeper into the heartland—pioneers, cowboys, railroad workers—were men and women who learned how to adapt to their environment out of necessity. When the land was settled and the frontier had disappeared, we didn't suddenly change our personality. We continued to view the world as a list of tasks to be tackled by American ingenuity. There's always a wilderness to conquer, as John Kennedy understood in 1960 when he proposed his New Frontier and challenged our nation to put a man on the moon before the decade was out.

It's no wonder, then, that our single contribution to philosophy (once our intellectual traditions began to mature) would be pragmatism, a philosophy that reflects these shaping national experiences. Pragmatism is the belief that truth is determined by its practical considerations, by its efficacy, by "what works." Something is true, according to the pragmatist, because it actually produces beneficial results in the material world, not because it corresponds to some metaphysical absolute. Formulated in the late nineteenth century by Charles Sanders Peirce, pragmatism was developed more fully by William James and popularized in the early twentieth century by John Dewey. The impact Dewey had on American education in particular has been enormous—judged by many to be a colossal failure of misplaced optimism in human nature. The classroom became a laboratory in which new "scientific" methods could be tested on compliant subjects. Content became less important than hands-on skills.

But pragmatism is much more than an unfortunate prank played on American schoolchildren. It's a serious theory of knowledge and truth. That's the most troubling thing about it. For the pragmatist—whether schoolteacher or jurist—what is true is always what works. The metaphysical (or spiritual) dimension of truth is canceled out entirely by the material conditions of the moment. This distinctly American philosophy has had a profound impact on every area of our culture, including our approach to public policy, our legal system, and even the American church.

Late-nineteenth-century America was primed and ready to take the cultural virtue of practicality (called "horse sense" on the frontier) and turn it into a philosophy. The rapid westward expansion of our nation and the growth in our industrial output required an institutionalization of virtues that had come naturally, instinctively, to the Daniel Boones of a previous generation. College curricula were retooled to reflect a shift in emphasis from Puritan metaphysics to the practical needs of research and technology, oil drilling and railroad building. Our legal institutions, too, were refashioned as Darwinian materialism made inroads into American thought in the late nineteenth century.

The career of Oliver Wendell Holmes Jr. followed the trajectory of American culture after the Civil War. Fresh from the horrors of battle (he was wounded three times), Holmes went to Harvard, where he was exposed to bold new ideas that seemed destined to shape the world. He embraced Darwinism and pragmatism and carried those ideas with him to the U.S. Supreme Court, where he served from 1902 to 1932. Holmes exerted a powerful influence on American law. Following Holmes, legal truth has been increasingly understood in terms of the end product that the law achieves in society. In law schools across America, Holmes is held up as the very model of the pragmatic jurist, one not bound to the letter of the law but free to interpret its spirit in light of present circumstances. Little attention is paid to the dark side of his social Darwinism—for example, his endorsement of eugenics, the view that society should speed up the process of natural selection by breeding out undesirables from the gene pool. When *Buck v. Bell* came before the high court in 1927, Holmes wrote for the 8–1 majority that the state had an interest in forcing the sterilization of a young woman named Carrie. Holmes punctuated his decision with a chilling, pragmatic, Darwinian statement: "Three genera-tions of imbeciles are enough." Horse sense, indeed.

It's uncanny how the ancient Romans, once again, seem to prefigure our own national temperament. Roman practicality, a character trait that served them well in empire building, was just another expression of a deep-seated materialism, an orientation to the things of this world. Rome sought to mark the material world with its image, as Jesus ironically noted when He asked for a Roman coin: "Whose image . . . is this? . . . Render therefore to Caesar the things that are Caesar's, and to God the things that are God's" (Matthew 22:20-21). The Romans stamped their image on their greatest building projects, such as aqueducts, public baths, and especially the vast Roman highway that linked the Empire all the way from Scotland to the Persian Gulf. Material goods, Roman armies, and ultimately even the gospel would travel along these monuments to Roman practicality. The gospel cut to the materialistic heart of what Rome was, and the persecution of the early Christians was therefore inevitable. Two worldviews, two kingdoms had come into conflict, and Jesus told His disciples to pick which side they were willing to stand on.

Sadly, we see this spirit of pragmatism driving much of the evangelical church today. For some, "church growth" has virtually become an end in itself, thus forcing a subtle redefinition of the church's mission within the world. Much good has come from the desire to reach the unchurched with the love of Christ. Powerful new methods of evangelism have been pioneered in the digital age. But the underlying mission of the church, and the central authority of God's Word, should never be sacrified on the altar of relevance. Paul certainly recognized that we bring the gospel to different audiences. He readily conceded the point that sometimes we must adjust our voice and even our vocabulary. "I have become all things to all men," he wrote, "that I might by all means save some" (1 Corinthians 9:22). Paul knew how to speak the political language of the Romans, the philosophical language of the Greeks, and the religious language of the Jews. The message never changed, however. It was always "Christ and Him crucified." The evangelical church has shown great flexibility in adapting the gospel to its culture, as demonstrated by the Jesus movement of the 1960s and 1970s, the seeker movement of the 1980s and 1990s, and the emergent church movement of the twenty-first century. But we should recognize the dangers, too—the tendency for us to look outside the authority of Scripture and beyond the power of the Holy Spirit for our foundation.

Pragmatism, like self-reliance, comes with a high spiritual price tag. Cain was pragmatic—and disobedient. God had demanded a blood sacrifice, but Cain was not a herdsman. He was a farmer with plenty of excellent crops to offer God. Certainly fruits and vegetables provided a convenient alternative to securing a sheep from his brother, Abel. After all, if he went to Abel, Cain would have to trade crops for sheep. Why not cut the middleman out altogether? But Cain's sacrifice did not please God. Nor did the actions of King Saul, who was also pragmatic and disobedient. The prophet Samuel had delivered God's unambiguous message to the king. He was to destroy the Amalekites completely. He was not to spare a single living thing—not even the sheep and cattle. It made no sense to Saul's practical mind for all those fine animals to go to waste when he could use them. Saul chose disobedience and forfeited his kingdom.

This spirit of pragmatism has swept over the evangelical church during the same generation that witnessed the rise and fall of the Christian Right. I believe this is no coincidence. These experiments in redefining the public face of the church are a reaction, in part, to the excesses of political activism. Two generations ago, fundamentalists retired from public life after Prohibition and the Scopes trial. History is replaying itself as a new generation of evangelicals reassesses the church's role in society. The wrong lessons, though, have been learned from our failure to transform American culture for God. The church may be withdrawing from the public sphere, but it's only substituting one pragmatic answer to society's problems for another.

Certainly, the practical tools of the electoral system have proved ineffective. Some people have been turned off to the church by the politicization of our message. But is our only remedy to indulge the emotional, material, and social needs of the world? Is this all we have to offer—either political solutions or feel-good communities? Is the Holy Spirit no longer active in the church? Does the Word of God no longer retain its power?

NEVER OURS TO LOSE

The values we identified as American myths in this chapter are usually taken to be distinctive and exceptional aspects of our character, ones that mark a break with European culture. But seen another way, these are the typical values of the modern age. The first settlers who landed on the Eastern seaboard in the early seventeenth century yearned to build a utopian community, a city on a hill. To be sure, this would be a community of believers, shaped by faith and obedience to a sovereign God; but this utopian vision would also be motivated by their own reason, effort, and self-interest. The competition between secularism and faith runs deep in our history, between the materialistic values of the modern age and the Puritanism of our colonial heritage. Histories of America have long noted this unreconciled duality. The culture wars of today, with their divergent views of American history, ultimately find their roots in this dual parentage.

The New World was discovered at the dawn of the modern age, and we've been trending post-Christian, like the rest of the Western world, ever since Jamestown was founded and the Plymouth colony was settled. The American experiment can be viewed as an attempt to synthesize Christian values with the humanistic goals of the postmedieval world. All the new ideas and humanistic ideals of the modern world—the dignity of the individual, the power of capital, the utility of human reason—could be tested in a world without kings and popes. The American continent was a blank slate on which modern man (a "new Adam," as depicted in classic American literature) would write a brand-new narrative of independence, self-reliance, and material prosperity. This narrative was often framed within the vocabulary of Christian thought, but it was a humanistic project from the very beginning. Humanism is the religion of the modern age, and the seeds of this humanism were planted in the New World when the shining city was chartered.

In a sense, America was never ours to lose.

CHAPTER FOUR

The Long Defeat

It is my strong conviction that only a pervasive and national spiritual

awakening can prevent us entering the post-Christian era

as we go into the 21st century.

— JERRY FALWELL

Marvin was settling back too comfortably, I thought, on my sister-in-law's couch. All night long he'd been strewing the conversation with rude asides about religion, faith, conservative values—even tossing out a puzzling comment about the "biological basis" of homosexuality. "You see it among *animals*," he said. "So all this morality stuff is just stupid bigotry." Nobody was talking about homosexuality except Marvin. Nobody was talking about evolution or hypocrites in the church or superstition except Marvin. We just wanted to enjoy the barbecue chicken—but Marvin clearly had other bones to pick.

My wife and I were vacationing in Southern California, visiting her sister's family and barbecuing that evening on the back patio. Everyone was enjoying the cookout until Marvin, a research scientist with a Ph.D. in biochemistry, started talking too much. Marvin knew he was in the company of Christians. If nothing else, the act of praying before we cut up the chicken probably tipped him off. But as the night progressed, Marvin went out of his way to make provocative statements, as though he wanted to turn the evening into a debate about religion and science, faith and reason. After listening for an hour or so, I finally responded to his cumulative insults.

"Perhaps you can clear something up for me," I began. "Why is it that research scientists, taken as a demographic group, disproportionately reject any belief in God?" Studies have shown that close to 90 percent of leading scientists at major research institutions profess that they have no belief in a personal God, that they are (for all intents and purposes) practicing atheists. The numbers are almost exactly reversed, however, when you look at the general population. The vast majority of the American public believes there is a personal God. They might harbor strange, even unbiblical, notions of who this God is, but most Americans don't seriously question His existence. "What accounts for this disparity?" I asked. At first Marvin questioned—but then ultimately conceded—my premise. He was unable, though, to account for this enormous gap between what research scientists and the general public believe.

"As I see it, there are only two possibilities," I said. "Either scientists like yourself know something that the rest of us don't and have been driven to unbelief inevitably by the simple findings of science, or they *choose* not to believe in God." I pressed him on this point, since he'd been presenting himself all night as one who "just accepts the facts" in a dispassionate, detached, and impersonal way. Christians like myself, of course, are the ones who allow our subjective beliefs to color our view of the world; scientists like Marvin base their conclusions on the sure foundation of objective fact.

"So what are the facts?" I pressed. "What are the findings of science as to where life came from? How did inorganic matter become organic? How did consciousness emerge?" Marvin ultimately conceded my point that we always begin with a belief system. We begin with certain assumptions about the way the world is. This is true for the secular scientist as surely as it is for the practicing Christian. Marvin wasn't very comfortable on my sister-in-law's couch anymore, and the long evening ended abruptly. He had been forced to confront what post-Christian materialists are reluctant to see: that they have swapped out one belief system and one set of values for another. He had chosen scientific materialism as his creed. It's something he *believes.*

The Bible has a name for people like Marvin. Peter called them "scoffers," and he warned that we'll run into them left and right in the last days. These are material individuals who reduce life to fleshly desires, who badger the faithful with the cleverness of human wisdom, and who deny the reality of a God who speaks and acts in the world.

> Knowing this first: that scoffers will come in the last days, walking
> according to their own lusts, and saying, "Where is the promise of
> His coming? For since the fathers fell asleep, all things continue as
> they were from the beginning of creation." 2 PETER 3:3-4

It's almost as though Peter anticipated the claims of modern science, specifically uniformitarianism, the belief that all things continue as they were from the beginning. The sun rises and the sun sets. The seasons come and go. Everything runs like clockwork according to the laws of science. Divine interventions into the cosmos—such as Creation, the Incarnation, the Resurrection, and Judgment Day—are categorically ruled out since they violate the predictable uniformity of nature. Peter stresses that the Word of God—not just the Bible, but the whole creative output of God—answers the words of people. The scoffers "willfully forget," Peter noted, "that by the word of God the heavens were of old." They forget that the world is "now preserved by the same word." And finally, they forget that the world is "reserved for fire until the day of judgment and perdition of ungodly men." Peter's emphasis is significant. *Only* God's Word, the "Word became flesh," brings salvation to our hearts. *Only* God's Word answers the emptiness of the secular worldview. *Only* God's Word is sovereign over the material world. The laws of science never will be.

Marvin brought a piece of the Western world into my sister-in-law's home that night—a preview of what lies ahead as America in the new millennium is increasingly post-Christian, increasingly hostile to faith. It's often pointed out that America continues to be a deeply religious country, unlike most of the nations of Western Europe. And this is true. One could say that the outlook is not nearly as bleak as I'm making it out to be. After all, I've been focusing on the minority of people, like Marvin, who are atheists. What about the 90 percent of the general public who do believe in God? Still, Marvin illustrates the leading edge of our future as a society, the opinion makers who are driving a secular, post-Christian agenda. This chapter tells the story of the long defeat of the Christian worldview in the Western world.

MILITANT ATHEISM

Marvin has a lot of company among the elite shapers of public opinion. Five hundred years of cultural and intellectual history have produced a world that is increasingly hostile to faith and all forms of supernaturalism. Something seems to have happened as the millennium approached. And now that we're well into the twenty-first century, we can see that a militant materialism has replaced the soft materialism of previous eras. This change in tone is most evident in the writings of the so-called New Atheists—Richard Dawkins, Daniel Dennett, Sam Harris, Christopher Hitchens—men who have been trying to accelerate a process that's been under way for centuries. This new breed of atheist intellectuals is prosecuting a coordinated war on faith in the Western world, and they're doing so with a missionary zeal. The titles of some recent bestsellers give away the strategy: *The God Delusion, Breaking the Spell, The End of Faith,* and *God Is Not Great.* In a style that is often ruthlessly vicious, the authors of these books round up people of every faith, color, and creed and march us collectively into their rhetorical gas chambers. The evil of religion—and the virtue of reason—is the unrelenting, black-and-white theme of these secular diatribes. With little regard to the historical nuances of their subject, the authors vigorously press the claims of scientific materialism.

Of course, this hostility to Christianity has been bubbling up in Western culture for some time. In the eighteenth century, Voltaire mocked organized religion, and Christianity in particular. "Christianity is the most ridiculous, the most absurd and bloody religion that has ever infected the world," he said. In the nineteenth century, everyone's favorite American author, Mark Twain, said that "if there is a God, he is a malign thug." In the early twentieth century, H. L. Mencken was brutal in his attacks on fundamentalist Christians. "God is the immemorial refuge," Mencken wrote, "of the incompetent, the helpless, the miserable." But the intensity spiked considerably at the end of the twentieth century, and even more so in the United States after 9/11. For secular intellectuals living in the "reality-based community," as they like to call it, the atrocities of terrorism were a reminder to them of the dangerous fantasies of fundamentalist religions of every stripe.

A hundred years ago, atheists like Bertrand Russell were fairly smug in their unbelief but felt no particular calling to proselytize. True, Russell wrote a personal apologia in 1927, an essay entitled "Why I Am Not a Christian." But Russell was quite restrained, even when chiding Jesus for the "defects" in His teaching, foremost among them a belief in hell. We flinch at the sacrilege, to be sure—and we certainly take offense—but we don't feel like a baby seal in hunting season. Russell was restrained when he might have bludgeoned believers with his brilliant mind and savage wit the way secular intellectuals today are all too eager to do. It was not saintly charity, but rather supreme confidence, that held Russell back from the kind of withering attack he might have unleashed. Atheism was on the march a hundred years ago. Unbelievers like Russell in England and H. L. Mencken in America believed that religion in the Western world was headed for the dustbin of history.

Russell concluded his essay with the oft-repeated claim that religion is mankind's most basic response to a fear of the unknown. It's a standard line—all the New Atheists repeat it—but it flows from a culturally conditioned view of humanity, not from a reasoned set of arguments. Russell's attack on religion is dictated by the old Enlightenment myth that portrays us as rational beings clawing our way through dark superstition toward the light of pure understanding. Most thinking people today, the New Atheists notwithstanding, hold a more subtle and complex view of the human condition. "A good world," Russell claimed, "needs knowledge, kindliness, and courage; it does not need a regretful hankering after the past or a fettering of the free intelligence by the words uttered long ago by ignorant men." Russell imagined a world in which the superstitious dogma of religion has been replaced by the rational precision of scientific thinking:

> Science can help us to get over this craven fear in which mankind has lived for so many generations. Science can teach us, and I think our own hearts can teach us, no longer to look around for imaginary supports, no longer to invent allies in the sky, but rather to look to our own efforts here below to make this world

a fit place to live in, instead of the sort of place that the churches in all these centuries have made it.

The dogma of religion, then, should be replaced by the dogma of scientific materialism. And this is the unfinished work—the post-Christianization of the Western world—that a new generation of atheists is taking up with such enthusiasm. Few of them, however, would describe their secular faith as a dogma or creed; it is, from their point of view, just the way the world happens to be for those who live in the reality-based community.

But the urgency with which atheists are bringing their secular gospel to the world suggests that this hostility to faith is driven by more than the self-evident facts of the world. The intensity of the appeal points to an underlying anxiety, what we might call the anxiety of the unexplained. Where Russell was confident (and wrongly so) that science would utterly clarify the world, these New Atheists *know* that science is falling short in its promise to unravel every mystery. Whether or not science will ever solve these problems is a separate question. Science has not yet unraveled the mystery of life, consciousness, and the cosmos, but this doesn't stop these zealots from acting as though it has.

In many ways, Christopher Hitchens is the most complex personality among these twenty-first-century atheists. He has chiseled out a persona for himself as an iconoclast, a smasher of the public images of men and women of faith—Billy Graham, Pope John Paul II, even Mother Teresa. When my former boss, the Reverend Jerry Falwell, died in 2007, Hitchens was quick with a venomous obituary, in which he depicted Falwell as a Chaucerian fool who probably didn't even read the Bible. Cheap shots like this reveal how little Hitchens himself really knows about the religious culture he lampoons. Like Russell, he possesses a wit that's wicked in every sense of the word, but unlike Russell, he is quite willing to set all civility aside. In *God Is Not Great*, Hitchens abandons subtlety altogether in favor of a full-throated and intemperate attack on *all* religions of *all* times. History certainly contains many examples of bad religious people, and Hitchens mentions them all; but his case against religion might be stronger if he conceded that some religious people, including some Christians, are sincerely good. If my view of a secular Western intellectual were shaped entirely by the caricature that Hitchens presents of *himself*, then I would probably conclude that secularists are ignorant bigots.

The book was reviewed by Christopher's own brother, Peter, who modestly claimed to be "no less qualified to defend God than Christopher is to attack him." Peter points out that his older brother, Christopher, isn't quite as rational in his approach as he believes. Christopher is quoted as saying, "I can't stand anyone who believes in God, who invokes the divinity or who is a person of faith." Christopher Hitchens is essentially admitting that more is driving his unbelief than the coolheaded, cerebral reflections of a rational man. For Hitchens, the case against God is always personal. And this seems to be an interesting constant in the lives of atheists: Many tend to be deeply unhappy and often troubled individuals. It must gall them that their intellectual inferiors, the religious rubes they rail against, are far happier as a lot then they are. "How do religious Americans compare to the secular when it comes to happiness?" asked the *Wall Street Journal*. They found their answer in an interesting opinion poll.

In 2004, the General Social Survey asked a sample of Americans, "Would you say that you are very happy, pretty happy, or not too happy?" Religious people were more than twice as likely as the secular to say they were "very happy" (43 percent to 21 percent). Meanwhile, secular people were nearly three times as likely as the religious to say they were not too happy (21 percent to 8 percent).

Dig into the backgrounds of those who have thrown the biggest stones against Christianity—Darwin, Nietzsche, Freud—and you'll find some personal grievance, some unresolved bitterness. I found out that this was the case with Marvin, too. Anger against God had settled into his life for so many years that it had fossilized into unbelief. Only after we'd been talking for a while did Marvin admit that he'd grown up in a Christian home, the son of a Nazarene pastor. Nobody had treated his dad right, he said. His dad worked hard, gave everything he had to the church, and didn't have enough in the end to cover the medical bills. Christians are hypocrites, he concluded, and he wrote God off in the process. It's a sad enough story that Marvin tells, but it's also a cop-out. This is not a rational argument against God; it's just the bitterness of an unhappy man.

The tracts written by the New Atheists aren't fringe publications directed toward a few intellectuals in San Francisco or Madison, Wisconsin. They're best sellers intended for the general public. The stated goal is to shift public opinion about God and faith. These books are part of a broader process that's been under way in which secularism has taken a militant turn. America is becoming a place where God is exiled from public discourse and where believers are supposed to leave their faith behind the closed doors of church and home. America is becoming a place where the bumper stickers on the car in front of you might very well single out your faith for ridicule:

A mind is a terrible thing to waste . . . on religion.

I don't believe in capital punishment. Look what happened to Jesus.

Forget God. Write your own good book.

Is this persecution? No, not really. Not in the sense that the early Christians experienced it. But this kind of mockery—and these grotesque caricatures of Christianity—reveals just how much Western culture has changed. At its best, contemporary society simply disregards how Christianity has been a positive shaping force within the world. The various political, educational, and entertainment institutions of our cultural life impose a collective amnesia on us, representing Christian faith as the enemy of human progress and happiness. At its worst, contemporary society intimidates Christians into silence by targeting our faith for mockery.

From the end of the Roman Empire through the beginning of the modern age, Christianity was the dominant institution in Western culture. Was this millennium an age of darkness, intolerance, and superstition as it is commonly depicted? Or did Christianity continue to exert a positive influence on the world even at a time when the church was corrupted by false beliefs and practices? Christianity didn't keep the political system of Rome from falling, but it elevated the moral and ethical climate of the ancient world. Furthermore, the church played a crucial role in preserving knowledge, fostering scientific inquiry, promoting cultural expression, and pushing the world toward positive social change. Still, you wouldn't necessarily learn this from the textbooks that are written today.

In many ways, Christianity has been a "victim" of its own success within Western culture. All the radical ideas and institutions that undermine traditional Christian faith today can be traced back, ironically, to a radicalization of Christian values. Medieval theology (of all things) helped to foster a spirit of rational inquiry that would mature into the Scientific Revolution. The church taught that when we apply our rational faculty to the material world, we are really studying the glory of our Creator. In the modern age, scientific inquiry has been turned into a weapon against our faith, but this was not always the case. Christian teaching also encouraged the proper evaluation of human worth and dignity. Admittedly, the church's record is a spotty one on human rights. There were considerable achievements, such as the abolition of slavery, but there were also deplorable periods of official persecution. (The textbooks always point these out.) Still, a "Christian humanism" is one of the church's undeniable gifts to Western civilization. Christian culture would prove compatible, too, with the rise of capitalist economies in the early modern era. The material prosperity that followed from hard work done in the service of God (what we call the Protestant work ethic) would foster a self-reliant spirit and a love of material things. Three secular beliefs, then, define the modern age—rationalism, humanism, and materialism—and each one grew in the soil of cultural Christianity. Secular dogma today asserts that

☆ reason is the foundation of truth (rationalism)
☆ humankind is the foundation of purpose and meaning (humanism)
☆ matter is the foundation of life (materialism)

These secular beliefs are the true enemy that the American church faces today, not the ACLU or Hollywood or the gay lobby. And this leads us to a third false assumption that evangelicals consistently make about the so-called culture wars. Recall how we analyzed in chapter 2 the false assumption of our Christian heritage. And in chapter 3 we examined the false mythologies of our national culture that we too easily accept. In this chapter, we'll see that evangelicals have wrongly assumed that this cultural war has begun recently, within the last generation or two. Evangelicals have greatly underestimated how long this battle has been raging.

How did the secular values of rationalism, humanism, and materialism emerge triumphant? And how have they shaped the institutions of the modern Western world? In answering these questions, we're going to start in an unlikely place—the American frontier, far from the intellectual centers of Europe. On the frontier we see the promise of all that modern society would become, once it had been stripped of tradition, authority, and even God.

THE AMERICAN ADAM

One of my favorite old films is the classic Western *High Noon*, starring Gary Cooper and Grace Kelly. All the predictable elements of the Western are here—the stalwart lawman and the vicious outlaw, the timorous townsfolk and the madam with a heart of gold. The story culminates in a typical shoot-'em-up showdown at "high noon," in which good triumphs over evil. Gary Cooper strikes his usual iconic figure as Will Kane, marshal of Hadleyville, New Mexico. As the story begins, the little town is celebrating Will's marriage to the beautiful Amy Fowler. But the joy is short lived. News arrives that Frank Miller is coming to town on the noon train and is planning to settle an old score with the marshal. Instead of riding off on his honeymoon, Will chooses to stay behind and wait for the fateful encounter. Amy has good reasons for wanting her husband to leave with her immediately. Of course, she doesn't want to see her husband killed, but as a Quaker she also rejects violence on principle. Will and Amy have their first argument as a married couple, and Amy heads to the station to catch the same train that will bring the killer to town.

Filmed in 1952 at the height of the Cold War and the so-called Communist witch hunts, *High Noon* is often described as a political allegory of what happens when good men and women are silent in the face of a great injustice. There's good reason to view it this way, as the screenwriter (Carl Foreman) had been investigated by the House Un-American Activities Committee and was blacklisted in Hollywood. But the film documents much more than Cold War angst and paranoia. As a traditional Western, *High Noon* reenacts some of our deepest national myths—the noble challenge of settling and civilizing the frontier and the competing claims of social order and individual freedom.

The pivotal moment comes in the church scene. Will bursts through the door, interrupts the service, and appeals for volunteers to stand with him in opposing the outlaws. "It looks like Frank Miller's comin' back on the noon train," he says. "I need all the special deputies I can get." But what he gets instead is a fierce debate. One parishioner questions why Kane hadn't bothered to be married in the church. Another wonders if this might be a personal matter between Kane and Miller that didn't even involve the community. A few speak up in Kane's defense. "Don't you remember," one woman asks, "when a decent woman couldn't walk down the street in broad daylight? Don't you remember when this wasn't a fit place to bring up a child?" But in the end, the church members resolve nothing and Kane leaves empty handed. It's important to note, however, that Will Kane is still respectful of organized religion, even if somewhat dismissive of its utility. He's no Richard Dawkins or Christopher Hitchens.

Ironically, what the preacher says can be read as a candid summary of the way religion is viewed in the modern Western world. Circumstances have reduced the preacher to a dithering, inarticulate coward. Evil is staring him in the face, and he doesn't know what to do. All he can say is, "I don't know what to say. I'm sorry." Empty pieties and endless bickering are all the church has to offer, when what Will needs is action. In that great laboratory of modern humanity, the Garden of the World, only the self-reliant individual can tame the wilderness.

Maybe Carl Foreman *was* just writing a fable about what it's like to be investigated by Congress and blacklisted by the studio bosses. But I see another fable here—one that plumbs a little deeper, all the way down to the core values of the modern age. Fable or not, what happens in the little church in Hadleyville presents a striking picture of the long defeat that Christianity as an institution has suffered in the Western world. If religion has no real answers for the human condition, then all we can do is follow Will Kane out the church door to fight our battles by ourselves. Once the shaper of civilization, the church has been scaled down to an irrelevancy, a refuge for fools and cowards—the kind of institution Marvin was sneering at from the comfort of my sister-in-law's couch. The church did nothing for his dad either, so he walked out the door like Will Kane to face the harsh world by himself.

We're at the threshold of a new nation, one that has left cultural Christianity behind, and we can't blame a few bad Supreme Court decisions for what five hundred years of history have produced. The same forces that have throttled the life out of European Christianity have shaped our own national culture. We've managed to disguise our humanism under Pilgrim hats and powdered wigs and coonskin caps, but we're humanists nonetheless. You see it even in Hadleyville, New Mexico, where it takes a man who's not much of a churchgoer to do what's right while the pious sit in their pews. This is just a story, of course, but it captures the great fallacy of modern thought: We're ultimately alone, and we hold our destiny in our own hands. Here, in the stark landscape of the Western frontier, in this great breeding ground of conservative values that would yield Ronald Reagan as its future product, the American Adam has no need for God.

Historians have long recognized that America can only be understood in light of our westward expansion. Not that this is the whole story of America, but it's widely accepted that our nation defined itself against the frontier. Curiously, the West hardly factors into the story of America told by many leading scholars. For them, American history springs from the Eastern seaboard, an approach that highlights our colonial roots and the early settlements at Plymouth, not the wide open spaces of the American prairie and the Tombstones, Dodge Cities, or Hadleyvilles of the west. The frontier was lawless, godless, and libertarian. As we've already seen, the humanistic political religion of Ronald Reagan would unite the Eastern "city" with the Western "garden." Still, evangelicals never seemed to capture the significance of the frontier experience as a laboratory for humanistic ideals—not as a pulpit for old-time religion. Students of American literature, however, have long known that the American frontier has played a major role in shaping our nation's values.

☆

Ever since 1955, students of American literature have had to contend with the famous theory of R. W. B. Lewis as outlined in his book *The American Adam*. James Fennimore Cooper, Lewis argued, was manufacturing a mythology for the young nation in the 1820s when he began writing his Leatherstocking Tales—*The Prairie*, *The Pathfinder*, *The Deerslayer*, *The Pioneers*, and the most famous novel of the set, *The Last of the Mohicans*. The central hero of these tales, and the first great hero of American literature, goes by several names: Leatherstocking, the Deerslayer, Hawkeye, Natty Bumppo, and (to literary scholars) the "American Adam." Leatherstocking would seem to be the antithesis of a materialistic man, uncorrupted by Eastern banks and European fashions. Cooper described Natty as an earthy man who might as well have sprung directly from the soil:

> On his feet were deerskin moccasins, ornamented with porcu-
> pines' quills after the manner of the Indians, and his limbs were
> guarded with long leggings of the same material as the moccasins
> which, gartering over the knees of his tarnished buckskin

breeches, had obtained for him, among the settlers, the nickname of Leatherstocking.

Like Daniel Boone, Leatherstocking is a frontiersman, a pioneer in the American West, which in the 1820s and 1830s meant the Ohio and Mississippi valleys. In the words of Lewis, Leatherstocking "seems to take his start outside time," and "his initial habitat" is "unbounded," an "area of total possibility." This American Adam, as another scholar put it, "was to be the archetype of a new society; the myth was to become reality. The European, becoming American, was to live freely in space and in harmony with nature. The ultimate success of the myth depended upon its earthly fulfillment." Cooper's frontier saga presents in mythological form the worldly experiment of America. In the 1830s, it was becoming clear to American thinkers that the Eastern seaboard was, in many ways, an extension of European civilization. For Cooper and the other nineteenth-century mythmakers, America would have to reinvent itself by pushing westward into the "Garden of the World," as the Western frontier was often called. America would be a new Garden of Eden, and its fictional heroes as well as its actual settlers would be new Adams.

There are many things wrong with this myth, not the least of which is the way it conflicts with biblical theology. The very idea of a new Adam like Leatherstocking in a new Eden like the American wilderness would have struck the apostle Paul as peculiar and offensive to all we believe as Christians. Of course, there is indeed a "new Adam"—but he's not one of the heroes of classic American literature. The new Adam is Christ, as Paul told us explicitly in Romans 5:14: "Death reigned from Adam to Moses, even over those who had not sinned according to the likeness of the transgression of Adam, *who is a type of Him who was to come*" (emphasis added). One of the enduring features of the modern age, however, has been our brazen attempt to create this new Adam for ourselves, right down to the false promises of genetic engineering and artificial intelligence.

Leatherstocking is a self-made man, creating his own history out of the raw material of time and space. As such, he is the embodiment of modern Western humanism, a character type not invented by James Fennimore Cooper at all but recycled from a body of modern thought and transplanted into a new environment. Cooper presented an implicit critique of materialism in the values of this hardy frontiersman, but this is misleading, as Leatherstocking certainly reveals an important aspect of modern materialism, namely the belief that a man like this—with all his faults—is capable of self-creation when dropped into the right set of circumstances. In this regard, Leatherstocking is not just an American Adam; he is a *modern* Adam, of the type first described over five hundred years ago by an Italian humanist named Pico della Mirandola.

THE MODERN ADAM

Six years before Columbus discovered the New World, a young Italian scholar wrote what has been called the manifesto of the Italian Renaissance, the "Oration on the Dignity of Man." Pico della Mirandola possessed one of the most brilliant minds of a generation that gave us many brilliant minds, including Michelangelo and Leonardo da Vinci. The great cultural rebirth that we call the Renaissance marked the end of the medieval period and the beginning of the modern age. It was an Age of Discovery—the discovery of new worlds and new ideas—and the possibilities at the threshold of the modern age seemed limitless.

After the horrors of the late Middle Ages—the spectacular violence of the Crusades and the ravages of the black death—the medieval world was culturally, intellectually, and spiritually exhausted. Europe was ready for rebirth and renewal. The fifteenth-century Italian humanists who walked among the ruins of ancient Rome were the first to call themselves modern men as a way of describing the new world they were building on the dreary rubble of the Middle Ages. They also coined the term *classical* to describe the Hellenistic legacy of ancient Greece and Rome that inspired them with its humanistic values; and then, just to complete the set, they called the vast "dark" period in between the "Middle Ages." From this point on, the modern Western individual would see himself as "the maker and molder" of himself, as Pico della Mirandola put it in 1486. Where the medieval world had been Christian, the modern world would be increasingly secular and humanistic.

Mirandola looked back to Adam for his prototype of the new modern man envisioned by the humanistic culture of the Renaissance. The "Oration" stages a conversation in which God, speaking to Adam, reveals the divine purpose behind Creation. In putting words in the mouth of God, Mirandola gives us a manifesto not just for the Renaissance but for the entire modern era. Here's how he sets it up:

> Then God took man as a creature of indeterminate nature and, assigning him a place in the middle of the world, addressed him thus: "Neither a fixed abode nor a form that is thine alone nor any function peculiar to thyself have we given thee, Adam, to the end that according to thy longing and according to thy judgment thou mayest have and possess what abode, what form, and what functions thou thyself shalt desire. The nature of all other beings is limited and constrained within the bounds of laws prescribed by Us. Thou, constrained by no limits, in accordance with thine own free will, in whose hand We have placed thee, shalt *ordain for thyself the limits of thy nature*. We have set thee at the world's cen-

ter that thou mayest from thence more easily observe whatever is in the world. We have made thee neither of heaven nor of earth, neither mortal nor immortal, so that with freedom of choice and with honor, *as though the maker and molder of thyself,* thou mayest fashion thyself in whatever shape thou shalt prefer. Thou shalt have the power to degenerate into the lower forms of life, which are brutish. *Thou shalt have the power, out of thy soul's judgment, to be reborn into the higher forms, which are divine.*"

Speaking as the Trinity, God addresses Adam as a creature of "indeterminate" nature, contrasting him specifically with the lower forms of life that are "constrained within the bounds of laws prescribed by Us." These laws coded into the animal kingdom are the instincts that cause geese to migrate and spiders to spin their webs. Geese won't suddenly start computing flight algorithms and spiders won't start weaving Persian rugs. They are limited by the nature that God implanted in them. But Adam is "constrained by no limits" except those he chooses for himself through free will.

There's a little bit that's right, and a whole lot that's wrong, about Mirandola's view of humanity. Mirandola has one foot still firmly planted in medieval theology—this is the right part—with its clear separation between human and animal life. Humanity is understood to be the crown jewel of God's creation, not the brute beast competing for sexual mates in the designation Darwin gave us. Medieval theologians spoke of a "great chain of being" that linked every living creature, according to its hierarchical status, from men and women right down to the last flea on the back of the village dog. By contrast, twenty-first-century materialists (and anyone who has seen the Disney movie *The Lion King*) see instead a "circle of life" that connects all living things.

Both worldviews recognize the rich interconnectedness of life, but that's pretty much where the similarities end. The medieval chain extends from God down through creation, but modern humanity has closed that chain into a circle, and God has been excluded altogether.

The Adam of Mirandola's "Oration" is a unique creature, made in the image of God, and in this sense, Mirandola is still a man of the Middle Ages. Ever since Darwin, however, scientists have been trying to close the gap between humankind's exceptional qualities and the rest of the animal kingdom. Evolutionary theory has become the great underpinning mythology of the secularized Western world. Like Rudyard Kipling's *Just So Stories*, new scientific fables are being constructed to explain every human behavior in terms of humanity's long evolutionary career. According to this radically materialistic worldview, everything we are, everything we do, and everything we think can be traced back to a common denominator, an evolutionary instinct that links all living things: the competition for food and sexual partners. The nobility that Mirandola still saw in humanity has been replaced by base instinct.

Even the most puzzling human behaviors (from a materialistic point of view) such as language and religion have been provided with complex pseudohistories. But little evidence of any kind actually supports these elaborate theories; they are supported, rather, by presuppositions layered on more presuppositions, like the proverbial house of cards. For example, MIT neuroscientist Steven Pinker begs the question in the very title of his book *The Language Instinct*. But *is* language just an instinct embedded into our neural pathways by millions of years of evolution? That question is never asked—it is merely assumed. And Tufts University philosopher Daniel Dennett tackles religion in the same spirit of Darwinian explanation. The subtitle of his book *Breaking the Spell* candidly gives away the strategy: "Religion as a Natural Phenomenon." Even what the Bible labels as sin is now explained away by evolutionary psychology as instinctive patterns rooted in our distant past. If women in Western industrialized countries occasionally kill their newborn children, this aberrant behavior is best understood (they argue) as a throwback to an earlier stage in the development of our species. One reviewer in the *New York Times* rightly described Dennett's book as "a merry anthology of contemporary superstitions," which is a nice summation of where the scientific and philosophical consensus currently stands.

Mirandola does affirm a high biblical view of humanity, but in another important respect the Renaissance scholar is thoroughly modern. This new Adam, standing at the threshold of the modern age, is "emancipated" from his Creator, ready to begin his long journey toward self-esteem, self-fulfillment, self-knowledge, and self-actualization. For modern humanity, as for Lucifer eons ago, not even the sky can be the limit.

> I will ascend into heaven,
>
> I will exalt my throne above the stars of God;
>
> I will also sit on the mount of the congregation
>
> On the farthest sides of the north;
>
> I will ascend above the heights of the clouds,
>
> I will be like the Most High. **ISAIAH 14:13-14**

Mirandola's God sanctions in Adam the very thing that He condemned in Lucifer—the striving after divinity. God defers to Adam's longing and judgment, which is an astonishing surrender of the divine prerogative. Why did God create Adam and Eve? Certainly not out of curiosity—not out of a desire to see what we could make of ourselves. Not to see how much glory we could bring to ourselves. And yet this is exactly what the God of the "Oration" is saying to Adam. Scripture, however, affirms the great truth that we were created to be vessels—earthen vessels, at that—filled with the glory of God, not our own glory. We are to be filled with the knowledge of God, not the knowledge of ourselves. Everything is backward in Mirandola's humanistic creed.

Adam is commissioned by Mirandola's God as the first self-made man. He is to shape himself into the end product of his own choosing, the "maker and molder" of himself. It's no wonder that Da Vinci, this thoroughly modern man, has been reborn in our own day as the hero of *The Da Vinci Code.* The Renaissance humanists of the fifteenth and sixteenth centuries saw their own lives as works of art, sculpted by their own efforts into something of beauty. What force is driving this ambitious project of character development? Not the Word of God or the Spirit of God, but the "soul's judgment," the faculty of human reason that separates humans from the animals. Humanism and rationalism—two of the central values of the modern age—are embodied in Mirandola's Adam.

The myth of human progress, too, is laid out in the "Oration" and given God's explicit sanction. This is one of the most beguiling myths of the secular world, since we *want* to face the future with optimism. We want to believe that we are learning from our mistakes and improving the world around us with better choices. Certainly, the growth in knowledge and the explosion of technology can lead us to believe that the world is getting better day by day. But Mirandola's God does not promise Adam that he will someday make iPods and iPhones—but that he will make a better person out of himself. We casually confuse the progress of our gadgets with the progress of our nature, forgetting that the thoughts of the human heart are continually wicked.

Just how far could Adam take himself? God tells him that he can even "be reborn into the higher forms, which are divine." But here's the most astonishing part of the "Oration." Mirandola seems to have forgotten who spoke these words to Adam. In a stunning—and probably unintentional—display of blasphemy, Mirandola takes these words from the serpent's mouth and puts them into the mouth of God: "You will be like gods" (see Genesis 3:5).

We can follow the trajectory from Mirandola through the Enlightenment idea that human nature is basically good; through the belief of the Romantics that the individual is a defiant, self-defining creature; through the Darwinian myth of self-creation by evolution (the ultimate "maker and molder" of oneself); and finally through the American self-made man. All these ideas are intertwined—and the germ of this prevailing doctrine of our own humanistic age is laid out in the "Oration." Mirandola's humanism would lead ultimately to the evolutionary view of humans as autonomous, self-creating entities, bound by genes and environment but not by a Creator. The Italian humanist certainly didn't see this one coming. When Mirandola's God says to Adam, "You will have the power to degenerate into the lower forms of life, which are brutish," Mirandola never thought for a moment that modern man would actually take God up on the offer.

Leatherstocking is about as far removed from the culture of fifteenth-century Italy as an American frontiersmen could get, and yet he descends directly as a character type from Mirandola's Adam. This embodiment of the American spirit turns out to be the embodiment of the modern world. He may be wearing a coonskin hat and porcupine quills, and he may be more comfortable in a forest than an art museum, but Leatherstocking's heart is fully turned toward himself. God has been marginalized. James Fenimore Cooper places the same limitless frontier of human potential before his American Adam that Mirandola had envisioned centuries before. Guided by his own freedom and ingenuity (Mirandola's "free will" and "judgment"), this new Adam has been set down in the vast American wilderness, where he could finally realize the humanistic dream.

America had its Western frontier, but so did European civilization in the fifteenth and sixteenth centuries. The values of the modern world would be chiseled out of the discovery and exploration of the New World—and the American experience is best seen as part of this larger process. That's what historian Walter Prescott Webb argued in 1952 when he proposed a controversial thesis captured by the title of his book *The Great Frontier.* The discovery of the New World in the fifteenth century, Webb argued, led to a boom of discovery, invention, and innovation that created the modern world. As Wallace Stegner has summarized it,

> The new world created the modern era—stimulated its birth, funded it, fueled it, fed it, gave it its impetus and direction and state of mind, formed its expectations and institutions, and provided it with a prosperity unexampled in history, a boom that lasted fully 400 years.

The discovery of land and, with it, new sources of wealth, was directly related to the rise of the shaping institutions of our age, capitalism and democracy. The closing of the American frontier around 1900 heralded a future marked by contraction, not growth. There are real problems in Webb's thesis, not the least of which is that we can trace many of the developments of the modern age back into the medieval period, before the discovery of the New World. Still, Webb rightly noted that America must be positioned within the larger patterns of Western history. The New World pushed the trend lines of the modern age.

Other historians, too, have demonstrated the important role played by the New World in shaping the modern age. Social historian Alfred Crosby introduced the term *Columbian exchange* in 1972 to describe the vast cultural and ecological consequences that flowed from the European discovery and settlement of North and South America. What was "exchanged" between Europe and the New World would ultimately impact the entire globe. Food, animals, and organisms made the journey across the Atlantic and then back again. Potatoes, coffee, venereal disease, and smallpox were passed between the two worlds. But ideas and values also made the Atlantic journey. Western corporate structures and European political ideas were introduced through trading companies— one of the most important institutions in colonial America.

The original Puritans who sailed with John Winthrop on the *Arbella* were "carriers of European culture, adjusting to New World circumstances." Lewis Perry has captured in that phrase the complex personality of America, grounded in Europe but experimenting in a New World. The first settlers were men and women of their age, European and somewhat medieval, but also forward looking and ready to put new ideas to the test. There was no template for what they were going to build. They brought with them no fully formed notion of democracy but only the old hierarchical structures of the late medieval world. They embodied the contradictions of the early modern age. Historian Kenneth Lockridge struggled to capture the awkward contradictions of this colonial culture in New England and came up with the phrase "Christian utopian closed corporate communities" to describe the social experiments in New England towns of the seventeenth century. This awkward term captures the contradictions of America: transcendent values straining to find material expression in planning, social experimentation, and civic order. The early settlers had a foot in the two worlds: Europe and America, medieval and modern.

Others have noted the pervasive links between the Old and New Worlds. Speaking of both Americas—North and South—Peruvian writer and politician Mario Vargas Llosa identified one of the key modern values that these early settlers brought with them.

> However small their numbers, however crude their representatives, Europeans came to the Americas with *a civilizational ideology that was unquestionably modern, even if embryonically so.* Among the ingredients of this modernity were a rational understanding of the universe and a new understanding of individual initiative.

The "civilizational ideology" that Llosa identified as "embryonically modern" is further described by Mexican novelist Carlos Fuentes. "The so-called discovery of America," he wrote, "whatever one might ideologically think about it, was a great triumph of scientific hypothesis over physical perception." Fuentes was a Marxist, and he understood the conquest of the Americas in purely material terms. European settlers had learned how to manipulate and control the material world, which gave them a distinct edge over the indigenous populations that simply perceived and experienced it. Llosa and Fuentes both recognized that a new worldview, even if in embryonic form, had invaded the western hemisphere. John Smith in Jamestown and John Winthrop in Plymouth were medieval men in many ways, but they were also the carriers of the early modern age. With them, and with those who followed in their wake, came the humanistic and rationalistic values that would shape our institutions.

America is a paradox. We are cut off from the Old World but still thoroughly connected with, and shaped by, the intellectual trends of the modern age. We are at once a deeply religious people and the very expression of humanistic and rationalistic values. Our history is indeed ironic, just as Reinhold Niebuhr candidly described it at the height of the Cold War. Niebuhr was a complex, paradoxical figure himself, the son of immigrants and a socialist who became an outspoken critic of international Communism. Niebuhr's views are not ones that contemporary evangelicals would naturally gravitate toward, given his liberal theological and political positions, and yet there's wisdom in what he said. Writing in 1951, Niebuhr identified the materialism common to both the Marxist worldview and the American capitalist system when he argued that the evils of Communism were "the fruit of illusions similar to our own." Niebuhr pleaded instead for a Christian realism, stripped of the easy acceptance of cultural values, one that recognizes (as one critic put it) that "men abuse power, use reason for their own interests, and do evil even in struggling to be good."

What happened in the western hemisphere was not something new but rather an extension and even a fulfillment of European civilization. America is not some aberration but part of the larger Western experience—a case study in modern materialistic values. The first sentence of Paul Johnson's *A History of the American People* puts it this way: "The creation of the United States of America is the greatest of all human adventures." It's also the greatest paradox.

THE GREAT PARADOX

These material explanations should make us uncomfortable. Why? Because the modern historical method explains history as nothing but the product of material forces. Civilizations ebb and flow according to climatic shifts, natural disasters, pestilence, and disease. Civilizations are shaped by the availability of, and the competition for, natural resources. If these explanations sound vaguely Marxist, that's because Marx was a materialist. He believed that humans are material beings who become the sum total of what we have or don't have. Of course, not all secular historians are Marxists, but they share with Marx the belief that humanity is the product of our environment, shaped by the material forces of nature. There is no room in the secular mind-set for the sovereign hand of God.

But is there room in the evangelical mind-set for the material world?

History is both material and spiritual, because humans are both. We are made in the image of God, but we are molded from the dust of the earth. Mirandola captured this mystery when he described Adam standing "between heaven and earth," of the clay but striving for the heavens. This is the great paradox of the human condition—just as it's the great paradox of the American experience. Our nation was founded by devout men and women but also by trading companies and slave owners. Those who tell the story of a Christian nation see only the hand of God in history. But the arm of flesh has also shaped us. Those who would "take back America for God" through political activism see only the righteousness of their mission, not the cultural values and tax policies that often motivate their deeds.

The great paradox explains the difficulty we have extricating ourselves from culture. As Christians, we are not just bundles of abstract spiritual truths; we are the products of the world around us. We are American Christians, Russian Christians, Chinese Christians, Indian Christians. We are also male Christians and female Christians, suburban Christians and inner-city Christians, conservative Christians and liberal Christians. We can't avoid this, which is what lends urgency to Paul's exhortation to believers of every age:

> Do not be conformed to this world, but be transformed by the renewing of your mind, that you may prove what is that good and acceptable and perfect will of God. **ROMANS 12:2**

The great paradox gives us a great challenge: to be faithful to Christ in spite of our material circumstances, in spite of the cultural forces around us. We are called to challenge the authority of culture with the authority of Scripture. Only God's Word, made alive through the power of the Holy Spirit, can renew our minds—as the story of Martin Luther reminds us.

☆

On a cold November day in 1483, three years before Mirandola delivered his "Oration on the Dignity of Man," a little boy was born to a copper miner named Hans and his wife, Margaret. The next day the infant was baptized in the parish church and christened Martin. He would grow up to become a priest, a rebel, a theologian, and a politician of sorts. More than anything, he would always be remembered for challenging the cultural Christianity of late medieval Europe with the searing truth of the gospel.

How did Martin Luther shake loose from the prison clothes of his culture? His life had been shaped by the very values and beliefs that he would dramatically reject. How does this happen? You don't just wake up one day and decide to trade in your worldview for something new. His conversion was a work of God's grace through the illuminating power of the Holy Spirit. As Luther taught through Romans, he was struck—almost like Saul on the road to Damascus—by the clarity of the gospel. He could not escape the simple yet profound statement that "the just shall live by faith." Not by works, not by the sacraments of the church, not by the mediation of the priest—but "only by faith," *sola fide*, faith in Christ and His sufficient work upon the cross. The opening chapter of Romans marked the turning point for Luther, when he read that the gospel is "the power of God to salvation for everyone who believes." Luther's challenge to the Catholic church ultimately involved a political challenge, but it was rooted in the salvation message of the gospel. Martin Luther was certainly a man of his age, an intellectual shaped by the culture of late medieval scholasticism, but he was also a man who had been freed from the limitations of his culture by the power of the Holy Spirit and the Word of God.

Scripture always assumes a distance between God's people and the world at large, and that distance must be defined at the most basic level—the level of our worldview. Regardless of where or when we live, Christians must always confront the deeply entrenched values of our own culture with the truth of Scripture. If we are to understand what it means to be Christian in America, then we must understand our own cultural history and how it relates to biblical truth. We must acknowledge our vulnerability to the cultural forces of politics, economics, and race and be ready to sacrifice our most cherished myths to the glory of God. We don't have to become cultural historians to do this. We just have to be faithful to what God has revealed.

Confronting and critiquing our worldview is one of the most inherently difficult tasks we're called to as Christians. A worldview is nothing less than the software through which we process our experience of the world around us. I'm always reminded of this when I experience culture shock, that "fish out of water" disorientation, the self-consciousness felt in another country. Along the banks of a holy river in Kathmandu, for example, I watched a body burning on a funeral pyre. I watched the family sitting dispassionately on benches, accepting their small role in the great recycling of the cosmos. I witnessed, but did not understand, the dharma that choreographed this social ritual. The Hindu concept of dharma does not translate easily; the closest approximation would be "religious culture," the values of conduct that permeate all the institutions and traditions of a Hindu community. I remember coming back from Nepal and asking myself if we didn't have an "evangelical dharma" in America that is almost as strange, just as pervasive, and (God forbid) just as unbiblical.

We need to be like Luther—men and women of our age (we can't escape that) who are transformed by the countercultural message of the gospel. We, like Luther, must press our values through the filter of Scripture. When I was in Kathmandu, it was easy for me to see the idolatry and fatalistic despair of a Hindu culture, with its caste system, its Hindu cremations along the banks of a holy river, its grotesque gods and goddesses. So, too, it is easy for me as a modern Christian to take a critical look backward at the dharma of medieval Christianity with its idolatry of saints and relics. But what of my own evangelical dharma? What of the comfortable, uncritical acceptance of values that are anchored somewhere outside Scripture? What of the idolatry of my own crude materialism? It is always more difficult, but no less essential, to question the world I'm most familiar with, the one I cherish and celebrate.

The belief that America is a Christian nation that has lost its way can blind us to the truth that this world is an alien culture to the one who has taken up his or her cross and followed Christ. We're not supposed to feel at home yet. We're pilgrims—the kind described in Scripture who are looking "for the city which has foundations, whose builder and maker is God" (Hebrews 11:10). America has always been a missionary field no less than Nepal or Russia or Uganda. As Luther was stirred into action five hundred years ago, we too should be roused from our deep cultural slumber to see the world around us with Christ's eyes. "Awake to righteousness, and sin not," Paul told the Corinthians, "for some have not the knowledge of God" (1 Corinthians 15:34, KJV). As we awake to righteousness, we'll see that there are indeed values we must stand for in this present age. There are indeed nonnegotiable values, such as the sanctity of life, that are grounded in the bedrock doctrines of our faith—not the shifting tides of our culture. The defense of these values should be an opportunity to point people to Christ, not distract them from the gospel.

☆

Toward the end of his life, Jerry Falwell was realistic about the challenge. "Look at the culture overall," he told author Zev Chafets, "and secular progressives are winning. They have been for fifty years, and they probably will until Jesus gets here and sorts things out." But Falwell remained a paradoxical mix of idealism and realism—much like the president he admired so much, Ronald Reagan. In 1996 Falwell announced from the pulpit of Thomas Road Baptist Church that he would once again crisscross the country, leading rallies in front of state capitols as he had done in 1976 and 1980. "It is my strong conviction," Falwell said, "that only a pervasive and national spiritual awakening can prevent us entering the post-Christian era as we go into the twenty-first century. Look at Europe. Our Christian faith came to us by way of Martin Luther, Tyndale, Wycliffe, Spurgeon and many other great European saints. Today, Europe has not even a memory of their Biblically-based culture of yesteryear. This is about to happen to America."

In truth, "secular progressives" have been winning for much longer than the past fifty years. Christians have been losing the cultural battle for a very long time—since the beginning of the modern age. We'd be drawing the wrong lesson from our "long defeat," however, if we completely disengaged from the world as though there's nothing left worth fighting for. Rather, we have been given a prophetic role, like Noah of old, to preach righteousness to our age whether anyone listens to us or not. And we must pick our fights carefully, taking our cue from the victory Christ won at the Cross. The Cross always brings us back to the beginning, back to Genesis, back to the factory settings of life and truth—the very values that were under attack in the Garden of Eden and that are under attack today in a post-Christian America.

PART 2

WINNING
THE
WAR

CHAPTER FIVE

Back to the Beginning

"In the beginning God." The first four words of the Bible are more than an
introduction to the creation story or to the book of Genesis. They supply
the key which opens our understanding to the Bible as a whole.
They tell us . . . of the initiative of God.

— JOHN R. W. STOTT

He was always easy to spot with his dark blue suit and conservative tie.
It didn't matter where you ran into him—around campus, at a football
game, at the circus with his grandchildren, or at the local Bob Evans res-
taurant—he was always dressed like this, just the way the public saw him
on *Larry King Live* or *Nightline.*

"Dr. Falwell!" I said. "I'd like to tell you about my talk at Harvard."

He stopped in the hallway and turned around to shake my hand. It
never hurts to let your boss know what you're doing, and I knew that
"Harvard" would get his attention. For years Falwell had nurtured his
vision of a Christian university that could compete on the football field
with Notre Dame and in the debate hall with Harvard. The Notre Dame
part always struck me as the fantasy of an obsessive sports fan, but the
debate team at Liberty University had in fact achieved a national reputation. Liberty's defeats of Harvard in championship debate had become
almost routine.

My talk at Harvard wasn't going to be a debate, not in the strict sense of the term, though it would involve a sharp collision of values and worldviews. "I'm going to be presenting the creationist side at an international conference on the evolution of language," I said—and Falwell's eyes widened. If there's one thing he loved, it was the rough-and-tumble of competition.

"I want to hear all about it," he said in that made-for-television voice.

As a young faculty member, I was eager—perhaps a little too eager—to let Falwell know I was doing my part to further his vision of training "young champions for Christ," as he called them. Falwell must have seen this in me. He was gracious and encouraging. He even mentioned my Boston trip as a prayer request from the pulpit of Thomas Road Baptist Church.

But what I saw in myself, standing there that day, was a work of God's grace. I had come back to my faith, back to the stark simplicities that defined the early church, back to the radical opening sentence of the Bible. *I had come back to the beginning.* My own experience has led me to believe that the evangelical church must do this as well if it is to speak God's truth to a post-Christian generation.

BACK TO FAITH

The young man who had been zealous for God grew up and pursued the world's wisdom instead. What had once been so precious to me had become a marginal afterthought in my life. I was becoming, in effect, *post-Christian.* After studying political science as an undergraduate, I discovered a love for literature and languages and ultimately earned a Ph.D. in philology. In one of the supreme ironies of my life, I spent years studying dead languages at the University of Minnesota in a building called Folwell Hall. That's *Folwell* with an *o.*

After finishing my doctorate, I left the academic world altogether and moved to Lynchburg, Virginia, where my family lived. My mother was on the faculty at Liberty University, so Falwell (with an *a*) had never been too far removed from my life. For reasons that are not entirely clear to me, apart from divine grace, I decided to work with my hands for a change. So I bought some equipment, taught myself to print, got ink under my nails, and opened a small shop.

One day a young pastor walked through the doors of my print shop looking for a good price on some church bulletins. Troy had moved from California to Virginia to establish another church (of all things) in the "city of churches." If you open up the phone directory in Lynchburg, you'll see scores of churches. Just counting the Baptist churches alone will take you to over a hundred. Where I was standing, though, none of those could reach me. I had grown up in a Baptist church. I was the son of Baptist missionaries. I had experienced disillusionment and slid away from my faith as a Baptist. In the wisdom of my heart, I couldn't see beyond my own experience. It took the foolishness of God, as it always does, to draw me back.

Troy invited me to visit the little church he had just planted, a nondenominational fellowship called Calvary Chapel. A few weeks later, that's what I did. He was a customer, after all, and I needed the business. But I went again, and then again. I heard the Bible taught in a simple, straightforward way. Sixty minutes of expository teaching. No flashy illustrations. No politics. No legalism. No light shows. Just the Word of God in all its simple eloquence.

Something awakened inside me that I thought had been lost for good. My will broke beneath the gentle onslaught of God's grace, and I reaffirmed my childhood faith in Christ. The Word of God, stored in my heart years before, quickened once again and I was able to see beyond the "hypocrisy" and "legalism" that I'd once used as an excuse for my spiritual apathy. God brought fullness, completeness, and satisfaction into my life. Within a year I had married a wonderful Christian woman. Another year later I was teaching at Liberty University.

☆

Two thousand years ago another young man, zealous for the law and schooled in the philosophies of his day, came back to the beginning. More accurately, Saul of Tarsus was *dragged* back to the beginning (see Acts 9:5) in an encounter he would never forget. In his letters to churches and young pastors and in his defense testimony before Roman officials, the apostle Paul always recalled the blinding light that struck him down on the road to Damascus. Paul never tired of telling the story. He managed to work it into everything he wrote and everything he said. Paul knew that the story of his conversion was always relevant, since God is a consistent God who works in individual hearts the same way He works in the world. That's why Paul always came back to the beginning of his faith.

Paul's testimony is embedded in everything he wrote. Sometimes it's pretty obvious, as when he gave a blow-by-blow account of his conversion before King Agrippa (see Acts 26:12-20). Sometimes he was a little more subtle in the way he wove that remarkable experience into the text. In his second letter to the Corinthians, for example, Paul wrote metaphorically about the light of the gospel—but you know his mind was traveling back once again to that dusty road where he met Christ.

> The god of this world hath blinded the minds of them which believe not, lest the light of the glorious gospel of Christ, who is the image of God, should shine unto them. For we preach not ourselves, but Christ Jesus the Lord; and ourselves your servants for Jesus' sake. For God, who commanded the light to shine out of darkness,

hath shined in our hearts, to give the light of the knowledge of the glory of God in the face of Jesus Christ. But we have this treasure in earthen vessels, that the excellency of the power may be of God, and not of us. 2 CORINTHIANS 4:4-7 (KJV)

How could Paul ever forget the miracle of God's grace reaching down and rescuing him? He couldn't, which is why the great theologian kept coming back to the basics. Paul understood that God's grace, however personally it may be experienced in our lives, operates in every work that is truly of God—beginning with Creation. Always the theologian, always the thinker, Paul accomplished something quite remarkable in this passage. He fused his personal testimony with the rich theology of the gospel, and then he cast it all against the cosmic landscape of Creation. With the imagery of light and darkness as his common theme, Paul connected three works of God that are different in scale but equivalent in purpose:

☆ the light shining into his heart on the road to Damascus
☆ the light of the gospel shining into darkened hearts
☆ the light of God's creative power shining into the darkness at Creation

The god of this world, Paul wrote, has blinded the *minds* of unbelievers. Even so, it's not into our minds but into our *hearts* that the "light of the glorious gospel" shines. Paul chose his words very carefully. He knew that the only cure for a darkened mind is a heart flooded with the grace of God. It's not through analysis, logic, persuasion, or education that we come to Christ; rather, the Holy Spirit touches hearts full of need and longing, hearts shaped by our Creator, to know Him. Until God humbled him with one blinding ray of light, Paul had been a self-sufficient, self-reliant man—a Pharisee confident in his own morality, working through the political process to achieve the end of the law.

The light that shines into our hearts is the same light that shone on the Damascus road. It's the same light that pierced the veil of darkness at Creation. "God, *who commanded the light to shine out of darkness*, hath shined in our hearts" (2 Corinthians 4:6). Everything is suddenly brought back to fundamentals, back to the opening chapters of Genesis.

The materialistic worldview also takes us back to the beginning, but it's a false beginning of random, purposeless forces operating in an impersonal universe. Against this bleak and hopeless philosophy, Scripture affirms that God is a purposeful God and that we are part of His eternal design. The materialist claims that we are nothing but matter, nothing but earthen vessels. Scripture tells us, however, that we are clay shaped by the Potter to hold a great treasure—the glory of God. This message has lost none of its power, none of its relevance, and none of its urgency. It remains the same message Christians must proclaim boldly and live humbly within a post-Christian world.

BACK TO THE CATACOMBS

Just as we must go back to the basics of our faith—the light that shines out of darkness—so, too, we must return to the simple example of the first Christians. They can remind us how basic the spiritual war is that we're facing. It's a war between light and darkness, truth and falsehood, life and death. We're not facing a cosmic struggle between relevance and irrelevance. Those are cultural terms, after all, part of the vocabulary of a fallen world that's passing away. The eternal truths of God never expire. Christians today face no new challenges, no new battles, and no new issues. We succumb to the fallacy of "relevance" when we view ourselves as a unique people living in a special time. We might think we've been given the burden of making an old faith new again for this postindustrial, postmodern, and post-Christian world. But we are still what Paul described to the first-century church: earthen vessels designed for the glory of God.

Christians living in a *post*-Christian world can learn much from those who lived in a *pre*-Christian world. We need to hear from them how bad things were under Nero, how precipitous the moral decline was in Roman society, and how little regard the authorities had for the sanctity of life. We also need to hear how indifferent the early Christians generally were to political activism as a strategy for addressing the world's problems. They didn't agitate for moral and social change, but neither did they retire into separatist communities—at least not at the beginning. Humans are political animals, as Aristotle observed, and the early Christians were no exception. They lived in neighborhoods and cities; they paid taxes to local authorities and obeyed the laws. They also spoke out against immorality of all degrees—not just in the pulpit, but before the face of emperors. (In the late fourth century, Saint Ambrose directly confronted and rebuked the emperor of Rome, Theodosius, for his massacre of a civilian population.) Even more significantly, though, the early Christians had the reputation for living out the moral truths of Scripture in their lives.

Since politics is inescapable—a necessary byproduct of our fallen nature—we need guidance on how we should relate to "the powers that be." Paul gives us that guidance in Romans 13:1-7, which is the most detailed civics lesson we have in the New Testament.

> Let every soul be subject to the governing authorities. For there is no authority except from God, and the authorities that exist are appointed by God. Therefore whoever resists the authority resists the ordinance

of God, and those who resist will bring judgment on themselves. For rulers are not a terror to good works, but to evil. Do you want to be unafraid of the authority? Do what is good, and you will have praise from the same. For he is God's minister to you for good. But if you do evil, be afraid; for he does not bear the sword in vain; for he is God's minister, an avenger to execute wrath on him who practices evil. Therefore you must be subject, not only because of wrath but also for conscience' sake. For because of this you also pay taxes, for they are God's ministers attending continually to this very thing. Render therefore to all their due: taxes to whom taxes are due, customs to whom customs, fear to whom fear, honor to whom honor.

To this central text, we can add three more passages—1 Timothy 2:1-4; Titus 3:1-3; and 1 Peter 2:13-17—which combine to sketch out a brief theology of politics anchored in five principles:

☆ God is sovereign over the political realm.
☆ Believers must willingly submit themselves to earthly rulers.
☆ Submission must be accompanied by honor and respect.
☆ Though society may change, God's standard remains in effect.
☆ Civic responsibility for the believer is defined by godly living.

First, we must acknowledge *God's sovereignty over the political realm.* Romans 13:1 tells us that the powers that be are "appointed"—that is, set in place—by God. Jesus made this point with utmost clarity when He stood before Pilate. "You could have no power at all against Me," Jesus said, "unless it had been given you from above" (John 19:11). From a human perspective, the crucifixion of Jesus was the greatest miscarriage of justice the world has ever witnessed. It is therefore stunning to reflect on what

Jesus did: He *submitted* to Pilate, a craven political figure, knowing that He was really submitting to the will of His heavenly Father. The example of Jesus does not mean that we should be indifferent or passive in the face of evil. It does not mean that we should not defend the innocent. It does not mean that Corrie ten Boom and her family were wrong to hide Jews in their attic. As we will shortly see, these would be foolish generalizations to draw from the unique case of Jesus. But it would be just as foolish for us to disregard what Jesus was modeling with absolute clarity—the sovereignty of God over human affairs. In light of Jesus' example, we should be extremely reluctant to challenge temporal authority.

The second principle flows logically from the first: *We are to submit ourselves to the authority of earthly rulers.* Paul used the Greek word *hupotasso*, a military term that conveys a sense of rank and describes how one person willingly places himself or herself under the authority of another. The same word is used in Luke 2:51 to describe the young Jesus on His way back from the Temple with Mary and Joseph: "He went down with them, and came to Nazareth, and was subject unto them" (KJV). The twelve-year-old Jesus had just confounded the elders with His wisdom—and yet He *subjected* Himself to the authority of His earthly parents. Joseph was a godly man, but he wasn't perfect, he wasn't all knowing, and he wasn't always right, which makes the willing subjection of Jesus all the more remarkable. Paul told us in Philippians 2:7 that Christ emptied Himself of His divine privileges when He became a man. This profound theological truth was realized every time Jesus obeyed Joseph with a simple, "Yes, father."

Interestingly, hupotasso is the word Paul used to describe godly submission within a Christian marriage (see Ephesians 5:21-24). The significance here once again hinges on a great theological truth. The relationship between a husband and wife is a picture of Christ's relationship to the church. Just as Jesus submitted Himself to the Father, so must the husband submit to Christ and the wife to the husband. Why is submission to authority such an important matter with God? Right from the beginning, sin manifested itself as rebellion. Adam and Eve resisted the authority of God. Cain, too, brought a rebellious heart to the worship of his Creator. King Saul refused to submit to the authority of God's Word when he made personal adjustments to the divine guidelines laid down by Samuel the prophet. Samuel told him bluntly that "rebellion is as the sin of witchcraft" (1 Samuel 15:23). Under the judges, Israel was in a state of perpetual rebellion. The sad theme of that period in Israel's history is that "everyone did what was right in his own eyes."

But submission is not enough. The third principle is to recognize *the importance God places on honor and respect.* A biblical respect for authority is contrasted throughout Scripture with a carnal attitude of rebellious contempt. God's standard is enshrined in the fifth commandment: "Honor your father and your mother." We live in a culture where authority is not respected. But from a biblical point of view, it really matters very little whether parents or politicians deserve respect or have failed to earn it. God commands that we give those in authority over us the respect due to their divinely appointed office.

Unfortunately, the belligerent tone of much conservative commentary is inconsistent with the ethic of the gospel, destructive of a civil society, and contradictory to the scriptural commandment to "honor the king." Some conservative columnists, for example, present the ugly face of self-reliant individualism through their controversial rhetoric. Despite their offensive language, however, some of these outspoken pundits have even managed to become the darlings of many evangelicals. They have cultivated the public image of "rugged individuals" bluntly speaking truth to a liberal, godless world. That would seem to make them natural allies of the Religious Right. But their poisonous rhetoric divides and destroys.

Concerning the Oklahoma City bombing that claimed 168 innocent lives, one columnist even went so far as to say, "My only regret with Timothy McVeigh is he did not go to the New York Times building." Concerning a liberal Supreme Court Justice, this same columnist said: "We need somebody to put rat poisoning in Justice Stevens' crème brûlée." There's a crude humor in this satire, to be sure, but there's very little honor and respect. And there's nothing of Christ.

There's a biblical corrective to this fleshly, corrosive spirit, and it's found in Titus 3:1-2:

> Remind them to be subject to rulers and authorities, to obey, to be ready for every good work, to speak evil of no one, to be peaceable, gentle, showing all humility to all men.

"To speak evil of no one" means to refrain from cursing, slandering, and treating others with contempt. As John MacArthur has noted, "We can never use such speech with a righteous motive." We are to be peaceable and gentle, which means fair, moderate, and forbearing toward others. In so doing, we are recognizing that God has placed us in communities and that He has chosen us to be stewards of His grace. We are to be "subject to rulers and authorities," not just through obedience to the law, but through the attitude of our hearts. We can disagree with our leaders and let them know of our disagreement, but we cannot disparage and belittle them without stepping outside the authority of God's Word.

Fourth, we should note that *God's standard remains fully in effect even though society may change.* God allows no escape clause or exceptions for our personal preferences and political platforms. We may exempt ourselves in the commentaries we write, but the apostles felt no need to put quotation marks around *submit, honor,* and *respect* as if the plain sense of the words must be modified to fit the realities of rotten rulers like Nero or King George. We cannot cherry-pick the laws we'll obey or select the rulers we'll honor. Peter was especially clear on this point: "Therefore submit yourselves," he wrote, "to *every ordinance of man* for the Lord's sake" (1 Peter 2:13, emphasis added). No qualifications are built into this command, which is indeed remarkable since the Christians Peter was writing to were suffering intense persecution. Some Christians today believe they are justified in not paying taxes, as some of the money goes to support activities that violate their conscience. To these Christians Peter would repeat, "*Every* ordinance."

Only one exception is recognized in Scripture, and that's when obedience to human law puts us in direct conflict with God's law. Scripture is clear, for example, about the defense of innocent human life. When Pharoah sought to destroy the Hebrew children in Egypt, the midwives protected them (see Exodus 1). When the authorities sought to arrest the spies in Jericho, Rahab hid them (see Joshua 2). Early Christians sought refuge as best they could from the persecution of Rome, just as faithful Christians hid Jewish families in Nazi Germany. Scripture also asserts our right (and obligation) to worship the true God. When the religious authorities tried to bully Peter and John into silence, Peter's response was respectful but firm: "We ought to obey God rather than men" (Acts 5:29). But even here, there's no license for mockery or contempt. (Remember that Nero was the emperor when Peter was writing.) During the Clinton years, conservative Christians were particularly prone to disrespect the powers that be, egged on by radio voices that have become guilty pleasures for many evangelicals. Scripture is clear, however, that God is not pleased when we fail to render honor to whom honor is due.

Our Founding Fathers, too, found exceptions and qualifications, but they don't measure up to the high biblical standard set before us. John MacArthur has argued that America "was actually born out of a violation of New Testament principles" and that "any blessings God has bestowed on America have come in spite of that disobedience by the Founding Fathers." MacArthur goes on to write:

> To some people, evangelical Christianity was a proper justification for the American Revolution. They believe they had every right to load up our guns and kill Englishmen for the sake of religious freedom. The truth is, the United States was born out of a violation of Romans 13:1-7 in the name of Christian freedom. That doesn't mean God won't overrule such violations and bring about good—which He did in this case—but that the end doesn't justify the means.

It's not surprising that MacArthur (who is no stranger to controversy) has been roundly criticized by fellow evangelicals for his uncharitable description of the American Revolution. David Barton, the founder of WallBuilders, has described MacArthur's view as bad history and bad theology. As an organization dedicated to "educating the nation concerning the Godly foundation of our country," WallBuilders is deeply invested in a religious view of American history. Barton is an engaging, articulate, and passionate apologist for the view that America was founded as a Christian nation. His presentations are impressive recitations of quotations from the Founding Fathers, early twentieth-century public school textbooks, and legal documents. But all this documentary evidence comes to nothing if the American Revolution was really a "rebellion," a violation of the simple teaching of Romans 13.

Barton's solution to this dilemma is to argue that eighteenth-century Christians in the colonies understood Romans 13 to disapprove of *anarchy*. In other words, one could overthrow an unjust government and remain fully within the guidelines laid out in Scripture as long as you didn't settle for no government at all. Many of the "heroes of the faith," Barton notes, "were guilty of civil disobedience—including Daniel, the three Hebrew Children, the Hebrew Midwives, Moses, etc." But these examples only serve to undermine Barton's position. In each of these biblical stories, the conflict between human and divine law is clear cut—and God's law always trumps ours. Daniel and his three Hebrew friends refused to obey the imperial edict that would deny worship to the only true God. The colonists, on the other hand, were simply tired of King George telling them what to do, and they were especially tired of his arbitrary, draconian tax policies. Mercantile interests, not moral conflicts, inspired the American Revolution. There was no curtailing of religious freedom in the colonies that might have justified civil disobedience. Even if there were restrictions on worship, as there were with Daniel, Scripture never authorizes *violent* resistance as a remedy.

In an influential sermon preached in 1750 in the Old West Church in Boston, Jonathan Mayhew tackled the "problem" of Romans 13 directly. If governments are ordained by God as His "ministers" to punish wrong-doing, then "what reason is there," Mayhew asked, "for submitting to that government which does by no means answer the design of government?" Tyrants are not God's ministers, Mayhew said, but the devil's. Mayhew thereby teased out of Paul the conclusion that we need not submit to unjust governments, though this conclusion, I suspect, would have come as a real surprise to the apostle himself.

Thus, upon a careful review of the apostle's reasoning in this passage, it appears that his arguments to enforce submission, are of such a nature, as to conclude only in favour of submission *to such rulers as he himself describes*, i.e., such as rule for the good of society, which is the only end of their institution. Common tyrants, and public oppressors, are not entitled to obedience from their subjects, by virtue of any thing here laid down by the inspired apostle.

This pastor of the church where Paul Revere would hang his lantern had found the justification he needed to become a political activist. He was a vocal opponent of the Stamp Act and is credited with coining the phrase "No taxation without representation." There are two problems with Mayhew's interpretation. First, who decides if a king has become a tyrant, unworthy of the submission and honor Paul commanded? Where is the dividing line between our responsibility to submit and our right to rebel? Have we crossed the threshold if the top tax rate is raised, say, from 29 percent to 35 percent? The second problem is even more puzzling. Mayhew seemed to assume Paul's ignorance of the ruling powers of his own day. The apostle was writing to Christians living in Rome, and he was fully aware who their emperor was. Still, Paul commanded the Roman Christians to submit! Nero was far worse than any monarch who ever sat on England's throne, and yet Paul placed no qualifications on God's command.

Fifth, *our civic responsibilities are always defined by godly living.* The ultimate beneficiary of our respect is not the politician but God and His reputation. As Peter put it, we must submit ourselves to the king "for the Lord's sake" (1 Peter 2:13). Paul, too, said that it "is good and acceptable *in the sight of God our Savior*" (1 Timothy 2:3, emphasis added) when we live as exemplary citizens. In each of these passages, a direct link is made between our obedience to temporal authority and the witness we bear in the world. Paul reduces our civic responsibilities to two key elements: prayer and godly living.

I exhort first of all that supplications, prayers, intercessions, and
giving of thanks be made for all men, for kings and all who are in
authority, that we may lead a quiet and peaceable life in all godliness
and reverence. For this is good and acceptable in the sight of God our
Savior, who desires all men to be saved and to come to the knowledge
of the truth. 1 TIMOTHY 2:1-4

Paul was especially clear about what's at stake: nothing less than the
progress of the gospel. The quietness of our lives and the peacefulness of
our actions should demonstrate to the world another way to live, the way
of Christ that is not bound by the strivings of the flesh. Political freedom
and economic opportunity are wonderful things, but that's not what God
desires for all people. He desires *spiritual* freedom from the bonds of the
flesh as people "come to the knowledge of the truth."

Paul's writings, too, bring us back to the core issue of our personal
witness. In Titus 3:1-3 he described behavior patterns that are incompatible with political competition.

Remind them to be subject to rulers and authorities, to obey, to
be ready for every good work, to speak evil of no one, to be peaceable, gentle, showing all humility to all men. For we ourselves were
also once foolish, disobedient, deceived, serving various lusts and
pleasures, living in malice and envy, hateful and hating one
another.

The contrast is striking. Paul was saying that "we ourselves were also"
people of the flesh who sought to assert ourselves and achieve power over
other people. That's the political instinct—to win, dominate, manipulate, and control. Kingdom living requires gentleness and humility,

self-effacement instead of self-promotion. This Kingdom ethic, however, is not an end in itself. Paul went on to establish the profound connection once again between our manner of living and the message of the gospel.

> When the kindness and the love of God our Savior toward man
> appeared, not by works of righteousness which we have done, but
> according to His mercy He saved us, through the washing of regeneration and renewing of the Holy Spirit, whom He poured out on us
> abundantly through Jesus Christ our Savior, that having been justified by His grace we should become heirs according to the hope of
> eternal life. TITUS 3:4-7

We are to demonstrate love, mercy, and forbearance toward others—since this is what God demonstrated toward us at the Cross. In this way, our lives become a living witness to the gospel. But when we strive and compete for power and influence, when we promote ourselves and tear others down, we are playing by the world's rules. Whatever we do "for God" through our own effort only renders the gospel of no effect (see 1 Corinthians 1:17). After this rich theological interlude, Paul returned to good works and drew out the linkage one more time.

> This is a faithful saying, and these things I want you to affirm
> constantly, that those who have believed in God should be careful to maintain good works. These things are good and profitable
> to men. TITUS 3:8

It is because we have believed in God—as opposed to a country, an ideology, a political party, or a set of cultural myths—that we are to live godly lives. And this is the sum total of our civic responsibility as believers.

☆

So if the early Christians didn't transform their culture through political engagement, how did they do it? Of course, by the power of the Holy Spirit (see Acts 1:8). But let's look at this from another vantage point, through the eyes of an agnostic British historian, E. R. Dodds, an expert on late antiquity. Dodds grapples with the historical problem of why Christianity took root in Roman soil, when it was just one of many religions, cults, philosophies, and mysteries that flourished in the Empire. In answering that question, he identifies four distinctive elements of the Christian message—each one as relevant today as it was two thousand years ago. Dodds takes a refreshing and increasingly uncommon approach by emphasizing the importance of *ideas* in the rise of Christianity, not just material conditions like poverty and social injustice in the Roman Empire.

The first thing Dodds points to is the *exclusiveness* of the Christian message. The exclusive appeal of salvation in Christ alone set this new faith apart from the pluralism of Hellenistic culture. The religious tolerance that was the normal Greek and Roman practice had resulted by accumulation in a bewildering mass of alternatives. There were too many cults, too many mysteries, too many philosophies of life to choose from: You could pile one religious insurance on another, yet not feel safe. Christianity made a clean sweep. It lifted the burden of freedom from the shoulders of the individual: One choice, one irrevocable choice, and the road to salvation was clear.

Christians weren't persecuted in the Roman Empire because they worshiped Christ. They were persecuted because they refused to offer their worship to Caesar as well. On the whole, Roman society was very tolerant, at least by ancient standards. You could worship Christ, Yahweh, Mithras, Isis, or Jove, as long as you didn't claim a monopoly for your particular god—and as long as you showed deference to the state religion. The Romans were the original pluralists. One Roman emperor, Severus (who died in AD 211), even kept a statue of Jesus Christ in his personal collection of deities. Paul directly addressed the religious pluralism of his day when he debated the philosophers in Athens (see Acts 17:16-32). Standing among altars to the many gods, Paul preached the one true God who made heaven and earth and who sent His Son as both Redeemer and Judge. Paul put his finger on the very anxiety Dodds was speaking of. With so many gods, how will you know which one is angry with you?

The narrow message of salvation in Christ alone has always been a scandal to the unbelieving world. A central doctrine of modern secular society is that we are to accept all religions as equal roads to truth. There is enough clatter of voices in the world already. Christians don't need to add to the confusion. The church needs to repeat with clarity and unity the ancient dogma: "Neither is there salvation in any other: for there is no other name under heaven given among men, whereby we must be saved" (Acts 4:12, KJV).

Second, Dodds recognizes the remarkable *inclusiveness* of the Christian community in the first centuries.

> Christianity was open to all. In principle, it made no social distinctions; it accepted the manual worker, the slave, the outcast, the ex-criminal; and though in the course of [the early medieval period] it developed a strong hierarchic structure, its hierarchy offered an open career to talent.

Where *exclusiveness* refers to the message of Christianity, *inclusiveness* refers to its ethic of social equality. God is no respecter of persons, and yet people in the church, when left to their own carnal devices, have perverted this truth throughout its history. The color wall that divides the American church into black and white is a tragic legacy of segregation that we have yet to overcome. But two thousand years ago, the church also struggled with equality; otherwise why would James have reminded the early believers that God is not a respecter of persons? Why would he have rebuked them for ushering the rich man to a prominent seat in the front? A central truth of the gospel is that we are *equally* guilty before God and we find salvation *equally* through the blood of Jesus Christ. Our social, financial, educational, and political standings mean nothing to God. As Paul's writings remind us, "There is neither Jew nor Greek, there is neither slave nor free, there is neither male nor female; for you are all one in Christ Jesus" (Galatians 3:28).

Perhaps the most radical declaration of social equality in the New Testament is found in the twenty-five verses of Philemon. This short letter derives its eloquence from its sense of urgency. Paul's letter is not the abstract musings of a theologian insulated from the world of actual experience; rather, his letter grew out of a crisis involving real people who were facing dire consequences. A young slave named Onesimus had run away from his master, Philemon, which was an offense punishable by death. Onesimus had since met Paul and come to faith in Christ. Paul sent this letter back to Philemon, a wealthy Christian, and asked him to receive Onesimus back into his household "no longer as a slave" but as a "beloved brother." A beautiful theological picture of redemption and forgiveness lies behind this story, but it's also a real story of how real Christianity cuts through the social barriers of a fallen world with the miracle of reconciliation.

The church would remain "an army of the disinherited" well into the third century. Origen (ca. AD 185–ca. 254) admitted that Christians were largely "vulgar and illiterate persons"—*vulgar* in the original meaning of "common." There were exceptions, of course, but Christianity in the first three centuries made its deepest inroads into the disenfranchised majority of the Roman population, among slaves like Onesimus, not among its privileged minority. The message emanating from the Cross was very different from the one emanating from Rome: Whosoever will may come.

When I was in Nepal, officially a Hindu country at the time, I asked the local Christians about the caste structures that had defined their society for hundreds of years. I wanted to know how these social barriers were viewed within the church.

"There are no caste distinctions in the church," I was told. Was this an exaggeration of the truth? I don't know, though I suspect the reality is something more of a mixed bag. Not even the early church was perfect, as James reminded us. Culture is a hard thing to slough off entirely. But the church in Nepal and India, like the early church in Rome, has grown rapidly among the disenfranchised lower castes. Those in the higher castes, too, are coming to Christ and learning to accept their brothers and sisters as equals. These real-world examples bear truth to the claim that the gospel is the power of God not just to transform individual lives but to overhaul thousands of years of prejudice.

The third distinctive Dodds sees in the early church is the *otherworldliness* of its message. Dodds understood that Christianity cut through the stark materialism of Roman society. "In a time when earthly life was increasingly devalued and guilt-feelings were widely prevalent, Christianity held out to the disinherited the conditional promise of a better inheritance in another world." Dodds draws on the same concept here—*inheritance*—that Peter used when writing to Jewish Christians in Asia Minor who were experiencing persecution. We have a "living hope," Peter wrote, because we have an "inheritance [that is] incorruptible and undefiled and that does not fade away, reserved in heaven" for us (1 Peter 1:4). Christianity brought hope to a hopeless world.

Hope always looks beyond the material conditions of the present, however bleak they might be, to something better that will be realized in the future. Jesus promised us that hope: "I go to prepare a place for you," He told the disciples in the upper room. "And if I go and prepare a place for you, I will come again and receive you to Myself; that where I am, there you may be also" (John 14:2-3). And Jesus said something else that was very interesting: "If it were not so, I would have told you." He tied His character to this promise. The hope that Christians cling to in a dark world is not a delusion, an indulgence of wishful thinking. We're not whistling past the graveyard of the world. Our hope is anchored in the character of a God who never changes and "who cannot lie" (Titus 1:2).

In the very act of burying their dead, the early Christians remembered that faith is "the substance of things hoped for, the evidence of things not seen" (Hebrews 11:1). The images they inscribed into the walls and ceilings of the catacombs—those burial chambers beneath the city of Rome—bear witness to their hope. In catacomb art, the recurring theme is the Resurrection and the promise of eternal life; the Bible character most frequently depicted in the catacombs is Jonah, the one who was "three days and three nights in the belly of the great fish," as Jesus said, designating him as a symbol of resurrection. The early Christians knew that their hope did not depend on some Roman political solution. It did not depend on more tolerant emperors or better laws. Roman Christians were a "moral minority" who had an unshakable hope in Jesus Christ. Christianity is not another self-help philosophy of life—there were plenty of those in the Roman world to choose from—but a commitment by faith to the eternal promises of God.

We are citizens of heaven who are making a pilgrimage through this world, as the old gospel song puts it:

This world is not my home,
I'm just a-passing through.
My treasures are laid up
Somewhere beyond the blue.

Finally, Dodds mentions a fourth "psychological reason," as he calls it, for the success of Christianity within the Roman Empire, namely that "the benefits of becoming a Christian were not confined to the next world." They fostered a sense of community, a *belongingness* that displayed itself in social responsibility.

> Their promptitude in bringing material help to brethren in captivity or other distress is attested not only by Christian writers.
> . . . Love of one's neighbour is not an exclusively Christian virtue, but in our period the Christians appear to have practiced it much more effectively than any other group. The Church provided the essentials of social security: it cared for widows and orphans, the old, the unemployed, and the disabled; it provided a burial fund for the poor and a nursing service in time of plague. But even more important, I suspect, than these material benefits was the sense of belonging which the Christian community could give.

John's first epistle tells us that we will be known by our love of the brethren (1 John 3:14). The early church was not perfect, but as Dodds points out, it was known for its uncommon expression of love in a harsh and loveless society. Christianity has always been most vibrant when believers extend their love out beyond "the brethren" to the neighbors around us—any needy person (as Jesus taught in the parable of the Good Samaritan) whose paths cross our own. Our faith is fundamentally *immaterial*, anchored in the promise of a better life; but one of the surest ways

we give witness to our faith is when we meet the *material* needs of a hurt-
ing world. Charity, in both senses of the word, should be a distinguishing
feature of true Christianity and, as such, one of the most effective ways to
discredit the selfish materialism of a post-Christian culture.

As Harvey Mansfield, a professor of government at Harvard
University, has written, "We know from behavioral studies that, to the
embarrassment of atheists, believers, or at least churchgoers, are better
citizens—more active and law-abiding—than those who spend Sunday
morning reading the *New York Times*." This should be our reputation
today as much as it was for the early church in Rome.

Sincere Christians want to bring us back to the founding of our
nation. But certainly God wants something more than this. While we're
busy trying to take back a culture that was always lost to us, the Holy
Spirit wants to take back the church and equip it once again for the unfinished task of making Christ known.

BACK TO GENESIS

The phrase "young champions for Christ" always sounded corny to me,
but I began to understand it in a more personal way as I walked along
the banks of the Charles River in Cambridge, Massachusetts. I would
be speaking that morning at the Third International Conference on the
Evolution of Language. My pastor, Troy Warner, had come with me on
the trip to give me moral support—and to see Fenway Park. I would have
a friendly face in the audience, but I still felt like I was reporting for my
own execution. Yes, I was anxious, but I knew that if I was to train young
men and women to go out into the world of business, education, law,
and politics to be a witness for Jesus Christ, then I must be that kind of
witness myself among my own peers in the academic world.

I had even less hope of coming out unscathed after hearing the lecture directly preceding my own. A researcher from Germany presented his work using computer modeling to study language origins. Algorithms were wrapped in suppositions—and none of it was comprehensible. When he finished, he was immediately confronted in the discussion time by a leading scientist. "That was the biggest bunch of hooey I've ever heard," the scientist said as a prelude to dismantling the speaker's complex presentation. Troy looked at me as if to say, "Good luck, buddy."

The science lecture hall at Harvard was a theater-style room with steeply inclining rows of seats. I walked down the steps, clutching my paper and overhead transparencies, and began my talk, which was ambitiously titled "Demythologizing Protolanguage." I kept my eyes focused on the paper, sensing that the only friendly face in the audience belonged to my pastor.

"If language evolved," I began, "then there must be a stage before language that is almost, but not quite, language." The entire paper, in which I argued that the evolutionary reconstructions of language were fairy tales and myths (those were the very words I used), followed from that opening conditional clause: *If language evolved.* Nobody was alarmed by the skepticism implied by those words. It was understood to be a rhetorical device. Not to mention, very few in the audience seemed to recognize the connection between Liberty University (which was printed on my name badge and in the conference program) and Jerry Falwell. But I was a party crasher. A creationist among evolutionists, as they would soon discover.

The origin of language—and with it the whole package of conscious human experience—remains one of the great unsolved mysteries of science. The evolutionist always starts with the assumption that the world is a closed material system and that everything is reducible to physical causes. Language is no exception. In keeping with this initial assumption, evolutionists have been searching for a material basis for something that is essentially immaterial and symbolic—something that has proved highly resistant to material explanations.

Here's what I mean. Animals certainly communicate in complex ways. Primates can even be taught a rudimentary form of sign language. But the ability to speak about things that happened in the past or that might happen in the future is unique to humans. In short, we have *symbolic* language at our disposal, and symbols always work by forcing us to think beyond what is material, beyond what is in front of us right now. Symbols allow us to speak about someone long dead, to imagine little green men on Mars, to speak in hypothetical terms about "the road not taken." Symbols allow us to think and speak about God—the Ultimate Reference beyond the material world. My question to my audience at Harvard was, "Where do symbols come from? This remarkable capacity we have to imagine beyond the here and now—*Where does this come from?*" For a linguist, this is no easier than the biologist's question about life. And the answer has proved just as elusive.

My paper targeted the work of a leading evolutionary linguist, Derek Bickerton, and his attempt to reconstruct protolanguage—"a stage before language," as I described it, "that is almost, but not quite, language." Derek Bickerton has denied that language, with all its complexity, emerged "in a single piece." His protolanguage theory is a sketchy reconstruction of how language could have emerged over time—vast stretches of time—as hominids interacted with their material environment. What Bickerton and his colleagues are really giving us, though, is a clumsy substitute for scientific evidence. What they're giving us is a myth. This is how I laid it out:

> We are to imagine a stage before language as we know it, a stage in which all the major pieces are already there, awaiting their own

embodiment in the technology of syntax. Reconstruction is a captivating game—but it's also serious business. Philology—which is my field of training—is all about engineering backward to reconstitute absent forms from present reflexes. The problem with doing this, however, is readily apparent: Once you get a taste for the game, it's possible to start believing that you can reconstruct just about anything. In fact, the less you have to work with, the better—it makes the final reconstruction all the more plausible.

Here's where my audience laughed on cue. *So far, so good,* I thought. But my "big reveal" was yet to come.

Even in my most secularized state, during my years of graduate school, I was never able to swallow the view that language had evolved. Looking back, I see a couple of reasons why I always remained skeptical of the academic orthodoxy. I had studied with a brilliant Russian philologist, a thoroughly secular man who was nonetheless quick to acknowledge the mysteries of language. In particular, I remember how he paused in a lecture one day and reflected on what we don't know—always a refreshing perspective for a scholar to take. "How is it," Professor Liberman asked, "that the farthest back we can go with language records, we find *more* complexity, not less? You would expect language to be simpler thousands of years ago. Instead, it's the other way around. How do we explain this?" He threw up his hands and said with a slight, agnostic smile, "God." And then he continued lecturing on the conjugation of verbs in proto-Germanic.

The other reason I could never embrace an evolutionary view of language was that I had read too much Noam Chomsky. One might not expect Chomsky to top the list of influences for a Christian scholar like me, but then (as language shows us) God works in mysterious ways. Best known as a linguist and a political radical who's been quoted approvingly by Hugo Chavez and Osama bin Laden, Chomsky is an atheist who does not doubt evolutionary theory in the least. What he doubts, however, is the kind of myth making that passes for rigorous scientific research. Often cited as one of the most influential thinkers of the twentieth century, Chomsky has argued that language must have emerged *catastrophically*, or (as Bickerton put it) "in a single piece." The irreducible complexity of language, like the irreducible complexity of life, doesn't just "go away" because we wave Darwin's magic wand over it.

Chomsky's skepticism has earned him the scorn of neo-Darwinian purists who have labeled him (and wrongly so) a "crypto-creationist." The belief that language emerged suddenly is compatible with a creationist model, but Chomsky is no creationist. That didn't stop me from mentioning him at the end of my introduction.

> I will suggest that language "in a single piece" is just what we must be ready to consider—even if that brings us to the kind of catastrophism which Chomsky on the one hand envisions with his "language organ" or that Christians like myself on the other hand envision in creation.

Here's where my audience gasped—audibly. The creationist cat was now out of the bag. I had uttered an unspeakable word. How would my audience hear me now? Would they still laugh at my jokes? Would they eviscerate me in the question-and-answer time at the end? Could I perhaps drag out my talk long enough so that there wouldn't be any time left for questions? Where was the nearest exit?

But I continued reading and even gained some confidence along the way. Occasionally I would see someone nodding in agreement when I pointed out inconsistencies in the evolutionary reconstructions of language. At the end, I was politely applauded. I had managed to leave some time for questions, after all. The questions surprised me—not because they were difficult or hostile, but because they were somewhat sympathetic in tone. I had expressed what a lot of them felt. Not that my audience was comprised of closet creationists. Almost without exception they assumed as fact the Darwinian model. But they also understood the element of fraud that I was exposing—and they seemed to respect me for pointing it out. I was relieved, but a little disappointed as well. Wasn't I supposed to walk away with battle scars?

Harvard University didn't repudiate evolution and return to God that day. But for me it was a watershed event. I was bearing witness to Christ—in the post-Christian climate of Harvard University.

"I suppose you feel like Daniel in the lions' den," the moderator said to me when my session was done. I laughed and made a generic comment about the importance of candid debate. But he was right—Daniel was a natural metaphor. The room was shaped like a dark pit, and I definitely felt as if I didn't belong there. But the metaphor made sense for another reason as well, one that the moderator probably never intended, one I mentioned in the e-mail I later sent to Dr. Falwell. "In fact, it *was* like Daniel in the lions' den," I noted, "because God shut their mouths."

Noam Chomsky, himself no fan of protolanguage theory, later read my paper and even used the word *enjoy* to describe his reaction. He didn't object to how I'd drawn him into the debate, but he did feel compelled to lecture me gently. "In brief, the first sentence of your paper," he wrote me, "just isn't true." Chomsky understood the strategy of that opening conditional clause—"If language evolved." Mine was a strategy that called into question what no thinking person was allowed to doubt, even if (like Chomsky) you couldn't explain how it happened, and even if (like Chomsky) you were honest enough to admit it.

Over 150 years before my talk that day, Harvard was still a recognizably Christian institution when Ralph Waldo Emerson delivered his own radical lecture in 1837: "The American Scholar." A young generation in a young nation, Emerson said, should throw off the shackles of tradition in every area of life, including religion. A key plank in Emerson's argument was that God is present, or immanent, in all things. "When [the scholar] can read God directly," he said, "the hour is too precious to be wasted in other men's transcripts of their readings." Emerson was not speaking of the God of the Bible, however. As one scholar has described it, "Emerson's god is an immanent god, an indwelling property of human personhood and physical nature, not located in some other-worldly realm." Emerson's address was so radical that he wasn't invited back to Harvard for another thirty years. But Emerson's vision of America has been realized. Now I'm the one, not Emerson, who's out of step with my culture. Emerson had to figure out how to live with his *doubt* in a culturally Christian nation. My challenge, by contrast, is to live with *faith* in a nation that was never really "under God." I took one step that day, a small one, when I publicly acknowledged my Creator.

My address didn't create any headlines—though I was interviewed for Italian public radio! Still, my talk was just as revolutionary at Harvard in 2001 as Emerson's was in 1837. I was affirming what Emerson had denied: the truth of a transcendent God who is not bound to human personality and consciousness. A God who is the author of all things—including language.

Jerry Falwell and Noam Chomsky.

It had been a long journey for me as a young champion for Christ, but in the end, I came back to the beginning.

CHAPTER SIX

What's Worth Fighting For?

The great divide between secularists and evangelical Christians is growing, not shrinking. This divide determines many, if not most, of our national controversies. Debates over education, abortion, environmentalism, homosexuality and a host of other issues are really debates about the origin—and thus the meaning—of human life.

— R. ALBERT MOHLER JR.

We were resting comfortably in bed on a lazy afternoon, my wife and I, falling in and out of sleep, when we heard the bedroom door opening gently. I leaned over and looked up, expecting to see my daughter checking in on us, the way children sometimes do when they just want to make sure you're still there. But instead of our daughter, Marci's round little face peered in through the doorway. She does that once in a while—surprises us, that is, with her unpredictability, but also her joy and warmth, her humor and odd sense of timing. Marci has Down syndrome.

We feel blessed—in a selfish way, I suppose—that Marci lives on our street and that our children are able to count her among their friends. They've learned to accept and value her for the person she is, and they've been learning in a practical way—even while riding bikes in the cul-de-sac—to cultivate a high view of life.

But children like Marci are disappearing from the world. New screening techniques make it possible for doctors to predict with a high degree of accuracy whether a child will be born with Down syndrome. And of those parents who receive what has to be a devastating prenatal report, 90 percent are opting for abortion over the challenges (and the rewards) of raising a disabled child. Elective abortion is just one step away from an active policy of infanticide. Administering lethal injections to disabled newborns is the horrible, logical extension of a practice—and a way of thinking—that sees those with disabilities as a burden to families and federal budgets. The Western world now stands ready to revert to its pre-Christian roots when babies were routinely "exposed," left abandoned in the wilderness to die. That practice in ancient Greece and Rome has been called "the great stain on ancient history." The reappearance of this practice in modern Western cultures is the great stain on our own "civilized" but godless age.

What's worth fighting for? Life, certainly.

Life—in the fullest, spiritual sense of what God purposes for you and me—is the prime value of the Christian faith, and a progressively devalued view of our life here on earth is one of the surest indications that American society is embracing its post-Christian future. Life is the most precious gift God has bestowed on us. It's the great nonnegotiable of all we believe. As the irreducible core of our faith, life defines both God's original act of creation and His ultimate act of redemption. Our physical life, bestowed upon us as the image of God, makes possible our spiritual life in Christ and the eternal enjoyment of His presence. The great drama of redemption is a story of life given, stolen away, and purchased back at great cost. A biblically based defense of life should thus point people to God's ultimate plan for His creation.

TWO VIEWS OF LIFE

The devaluation of life in the modern Western world is tragic, but it's not surprising. The materialistic worldview is a brutal master that wrenches every last ounce of life from its subjects. Nature is "red in tooth and claw," in Tennyson's memorable phrase, and we get along best in this world (we're told by some) if we shed our sentimental attachment to those old figments of our imagination, like *God*, and *faith*, and *meaning*. This bleak worldview has been a long time in the making, but it's marked by three basic doctrines about life—and each of these is grounded in evolutionary theory.

First, the materialist believes that *life is reducible to chemistry and biology*. The belief that all reality is expressible in physical terms and is accessible to scientific analysis is known as reductionism. The universe is reduced to pure physical law, a view stated clearly in the opening sentence of Carl Sagan's popular *Cosmos* (1980): "The Cosmos is all that is or ever was or ever will be." The origin and progress of life, too, has a purely material basis. The spark of life did not occur, as Michelangelo beautifully depicted it, when God's finger touched Adam's. Life resulted from accidental chemical reactions. But what nature produced by accident, the deliberate and sophisticated experimentation of science has been unable to repeat.

The most vocal spokesman for Darwinian materialism today is Richard Dawkins, a British zoologist, author, and outspoken atheist. In one of his many works of Darwinian apologetics, *River Out of Eden*, Dawkins sneers at the idea that there is some abstract, metaphysical thing as *life*. "There is no spirit-driven life force, no throbbing, heaving, pullulating, protoplasmic, mystic jelly," he wrote, as though *that's* what Christians mean by the term. "Life is just bytes and bytes and bytes of digital information." Digital information, we might add, that programmed itself.

If we are nothing but bytes of digital information, then there is no larger purpose to life beyond the chemical and biological codes themselves. Life is thus reduced to neural firings in my brain and hormonal changes that flow through my bloodstream. Life becomes the sum total of my experiences, lived out on a purely sensory level. My goal in life, then, should be to live for today and string together as many cool experiences as I can possibly arrange. The materialist view of life implies that raw experience is all that life could ever offer me.

Second, the materialist believes that *the meaningfulness of life is constructed within a social environment.* If we are not created in the image of God, then where does our worth and dignity come from? Who affirms our existence? Society does. The community you are born into retains the power to confer life, personhood, and meaning on you. That doesn't bode well, of course, for the unborn child, the disabled infant, the inconvenient elderly, or the suffering cancer patient. When an individual's life ceases to hold any material benefit to society, then what prevents society from redesignating that individual as a nonperson? Can lives be so easily tossed away as a petty inconvenience?

Consider the case of Jennifer Raper and her two-year-old daughter. In March 2007 a forty-five-year-old woman in Boston filed a malpractice lawsuit against two Planned Parenthood doctors. Jennifer Raper's legal complaint stated that she had sought an abortion in March 2004 for financial reasons and that the abortion clinic botched the procedure. Several months later Raper discovered that she was still pregnant and delivered a healthy baby girl. Her suit demanded compensation for the costs of raising her unwanted child. There's a perverse "logic" to this case. After all, the law allows for the termination of life for personal convenience, and she had been inconvenienced by the medical malpractice and the little girl who entered her life. It matters very little to the cold calculus of a material world that Jennifer Raper's "inconvenience" is a child who loves to laugh and play, who giggles when she's tickled. A little girl who will scribble with crayons and give her drawings to her mother to put on the refrigerator. A little girl who would like to grow up into a woman with hopes and dreams for a good life. Society has the power to invalidate these joys, hopes, and dreams through a single judicial stroke.

Third, materialists emphasize that *life is dependent on death.* When I was growing up in the 1960s, I remember the cruel drama of nature playing out each Sunday afternoon on *Mutual of Omaha's Wild Kingdom.* I hated seeing the newborn antelope getting picked off by a pack of hyenas. The voice-over narration was so analytical, so detached. But I couldn't bear to watch. I wanted the fuzzy little animal to get its legs underneath it, to run, and to play. To *live.* I see no comfort in a world where life is sustained by death. That's not what God intended. The comfort of believers has always been the hope and promise of life. I love the picture of the "peaceable kingdom" that American folk painter Edward Hicks gave us—the picture of the lion and the lamb, but also of settlers and Indians, not killing each other in a brutal struggle for survival and dominance, but *living* together, living at peace. We see this millennial kingdom as well in the catacomb art of the early church, only without the Indians, of course. The Christian message is a celebration of life, not death. The doctrine of the resurrection therefore occupies a central place in the Christian's worldview.

> Death is swallowed up in victory. O death, where is thy sting? O
> grave, where is thy victory?   1 CORINTHIANS 15:54-55 (KJV)

It matters deeply that Jesus rose from the dead, since death could not triumph in a universe of God's making.

How does the Bible answer this impoverished, dead-end view of life?

First, the Bible affirms that *God is life.* This does not mean that God is identical with nature. We don't find God inhabiting every living thing, as the pantheist believes, or as Emerson and Thoreau taught, or as New Age spiritualism asserts. God is wholly transcendent of His creation. Life does flow from God's very nature, and in some way—some mysterious way that we don't fully comprehend—all life is a reflection of our Maker. Paul declared in Colossians 3:4 that "Christ . . . is our life." Paul echoed what Greek poets had said: "In Him we live and move and have our being" (Acts 17:28). To say that God is life is to acknowledge His primacy, to recognize that "every good gift and every perfect gift," foremost among them the gift of life, "comes down from the Father of lights" (James 1:17).

Second, the Word of God declares that *life is purposeful.* The controversy about the origin of life is thus of foundational importance; it matters whether or not life originated in a primordial stew or in the eternal counsels of God. If we created ourselves through eons of interaction with our environment, then we are accountable to nobody but ourselves. Scripture affirms, rather, that we were created for His glory. In Isaiah 43:1, God spoke to His people, the children of Israel, the house of Jacob:

> Thus says the LORD, who created you, O Jacob, and He who formed you, O Israel: "Fear not, for I have redeemed you; I have called you by your name; you are Mine."

God reminds us through the prophet that there is great comfort in knowing that God formed us: "Fear not," Isaiah recorded, "for I am with you" (Isaiah 43:5). God's promise back then to a scattered and persecuted nation is the same promise now to a scattered and persecuted church: "I am with you."

Everyone who is called by My name, whom I have created for My glory; I have formed him, yes, I have made him. ISAIAH 43:7

These verses give us a peek into the eternal purposes of God. Paul restated this great truth in Romans 9:20-23. We are clay, Paul reminded us, and God is the Potter, fashioning us so "that He might make known the riches of His glory on the vessels of mercy, which He had prepared beforehand for glory." If Christians fail to understand and articulate the grand purpose behind creation, then none of what we say about life will ever matter.

Even Thomas Jefferson, the great hero of the ACLU, affirmed God's creatorship in that famous sentence in the Declaration of Independence. For all his skepticism about the supernatural elements of Scripture, Jefferson would never have doubted, as he was dipping his quill into the inkwell, that the Almighty had started the whole process off with a purposeful creative act.

We hold these truths to be self-evident, that all men are created equal, that they are endowed by their Creator with certain unalienable Rights, that among these are Life, Liberty and the pursuit of Happiness.

Men and women were programmed by God to seek a purposeful life, what Jefferson called "the pursuit of Happiness." Jefferson was introducing a philosophical idea here, not a license to pursue pleasure. His phrase roughly corresponds to what the ancient Greek philosophers understood to be the virtuous life or the life well lived. Knowing that we were created for God's glory, Christians (of all people) should know the meaning of a life well lived, the happy life that philosophers from ancient times have been seeking to define. All that Jefferson asserted rests on a self-evident fact. He may have been a deist, but he was no materialist. Jefferson believed that our Creator intended our lives to have meaning.

Third, the message of Scripture is that *God desires for us an abundant life.* "I have come that they may have life," Jesus said, "and that they may have it more abundantly" (John 10:10). In the same sermon Jesus described Himself as the Good Shepherd. There's a significant connection between these two statements, since abundant living flows from our acceptance of Christ's lordship as the Shepherd of our lives. He is our provider and protector, the One who prepares for us the green pastures of Psalm 23. Since our Good Shepherd lays down His life for the sheep, abundant living has its origin in deep, sacrificial love, not the vain pursuit of the world.

Life is the great issue the church cut its public policy teeth on many centuries ago, and it should remain for us the defining value we show to the world. We must be identified with the beauty and sanctity of God's most precious gift, just as the ancient Christians denounced the gladiatorial shows and the practices of abortion and infanticide. The commitment of the early Christians to life is everywhere on display in the ancient Roman catacombs. Early Christian burial inscriptions also give witness to this, such as the one for the Egyptian monk Schenute, which recognizes that God is the One who "has graciously bestowed life upon the world." Life is not a right to be grasped in my hand, but a gracious gift bestowed by a loving God. A life lived with this godly attitude of humility and thankfulness will challenge—more than any argument could ever do—the selfish materialism of the evolutionary worldview.

Few figures of the modern age have cast a darker shadow over our world than Charles Darwin. It's ironic that the controversy about origins should be so central today, since this was the very issue that persuaded many Christians in the twentieth century to stay out of politics altogether. Jerry Falwell, for example, wrote in his autobiography that he was naturally reluctant to engage the political system in part because of the disastrous legacy of the Scopes trial in 1925. And yet we cannot separate the *origin* of life from the *value* of life. Very different policy positions will flow from these separate worldviews. As R. Albert Mohler Jr. puts it, "Debates over education, abortion, environmentalism, homosexuality and a host of other issues are really debates about the origin—and thus the meaning—of human life." One of those debates, inevitably, concerns whether you view the fetus in the womb as a human life or a mass of unviable tissue. That was the question that nine men in black robes wrestled with in the winter of 1972.

THE BEACHHEAD OF ABORTION

On January 23, 1973, the *New York Times* had one of those difficult days when there was so much news and so little space on the front page. The former president of the United States Lyndon Johnson had died of a massive heart attack—but the Supreme Court had also handed down a controversial decision on abortion. Two major political events, but only one of them, the decision known as *Roe v. Wade*, continues to shape American politics over three decades later. In the end, the *New York Times* gave the top headline to the former president:

LYNDON JOHNSON, 36TH PRESIDENT, IS DEAD;
WAS ARCHITECT OF 'GREAT SOCIETY' PROGRAM

Beneath that banner, in smaller type, ran the second headline of the day:

High Court Rules Abortion Legal the First 3 Months

It would take a few years for the full impact of *Roe v. Wade* to register with evangelicals, but when it finally did sink in, abortion would become the spark behind evangelical activism. The very best—and the very worst—

that we can say about the Religious Right is on display in the story of the modern pro-life movement.

It would take a gray-haired philosopher with a goatee, a Presbyterian minister who wore knickerbockers and lived in Switzerland, to rouse evangelicals from their slumber and confront the moral challenges of Western culture. Until his book *How Should We Then Live?* hit Christian bookstores in 1976, Francis Schaeffer was known largely to evangelicals through his philosophical writings on modernism. This one book, however, would extend his influence far beyond the college intellectuals he was used to ministering to at his countercultural retreat in Switzerland, the L'Abri Fellowship. In his sketch of "the rise and decline of Western thought and culture" (as the book is subtitled), Schaeffer would provide a framework for challenging the humanistic underpinnings of American society. Where Hal Lindsey had given evangelicals a foreign policy, Schaeffer gave them a philosophy of culture—and a reasoned argument for political action. Many of the leading figures of the New Right would acknowledge the important role Schaeffer played in motivating them to political action: John Whitehead, lawyer and founder of the Rutherford Institute; Randall Terry, the controversial director of Operation Rescue; Bill Bright of Campus Crusade for Christ; and Pat Robertson of *The 700 Club*. Perhaps Schaeffer's biggest "convert," though, would be the Reverend Jerry Falwell, who admitted in his 1987 autobiography that he had been convicted by Schaeffer's writings on abortion.

Of course, the abortion issue did not first appear in 1973. Ever since the church was established two thousand years ago in the darkness of the Roman Empire, Christians have lifted their voices in defense of the defenseless. Schaeffer realized this, and it provided him with a historical grid for arguing that the church had a righteous position on life, one framed by the law of God and not the dictates of culture. Abortion was a common procedure in the ancient world, for the same reasons of personal and public convenience that it is today. It was not universally sanctioned, however. History's most famous physician, the ancient Greek Hippocrates, charged in his oath that doctors should not administer abortion potions to women. The early church fathers were consistent in their opposition to this heathen practice. Basil was a leading pro-life activist in the fourth century, organizing public protests against abortion and providing aid to poor women who were pregnant. In 374 Basil's efforts helped to persuade Emperor Valentinian to outlaw abortion in the Roman Empire.

If abortion was so common in the Greco-Roman world, and if it's so clearly wrong according to a worldview that promotes life, then why doesn't the Bible address it directly? In all likelihood, Scripture does address abortion, but in ways that have slipped past our cultural ears. The Greek word *pharmakeia* is used in Galatians 5:20 and Revelation 21:8, and is usually translated as "witchcraft" or "sorcery." The word literally describes the potions involved in these practices. Herbal concoctions were a common method of inducing abortion in the ancient world, and it is thus very likely that a Greek or Roman Christian two thousand years ago would have understood the term to include this widespread practice. Some of the earliest extrabiblical writings we have, such as the *Didache* (AD 100–120) are even more direct: "Thou shalt not procure abortion, nor shalt thou kill that which is begotten."

Abortion is an ancient sin, widespread in the cultures of the world. The great philosophers of ancient Greece, Plato and Aristotle, even approved abortion as a population-control measure. But where the Greek philosophers had formulated a civic argument for abortion, *Roe v. Wade* is rooted in a modern conception of individual rights. The ruling, as

Schaeffer noted, revolves around an arbitrary definition of viability as the boundary line separating a person from a nonperson.

> By the ruling of the Supreme Court, the unborn baby is not counted as a person. In our day, quite rightly, there has been a hue and cry against some of our ancestors' cruel viewing of the black slave as a nonperson. This was horrible indeed—an act of hypocrisy as well as cruelty. But now, by an arbitrary absolute brought in on the humanist flow, millions of unborn babies of every color of skin are equally by law declared nonpersons. Surely this, too, must be seen as an act of hypocrisy.

Schaeffer's explicit analogy between slaves and the unborn was an effective stroke—philosophically sound, as he anchors his argument in the concept of personhood, but culturally incisive too, in ways he probably never anticipated. Schaeffer was shaming the very evangelicals he was calling to action. He challenged them to think consistently about life as the sacred gift of our Creator. Indeed, an unintended consequence of the pro-life movement may have been greater racial understanding on the part of conservative Christians. Fundamentalists and evangelicals could not remain insensitive to the legacies of slavery, such as segregation, and oppose abortion with any conviction. These grotesque social practices were profound violations of human worth and dignity. To view it otherwise would be, in Schaeffer's words, "an act of hypocrisy."

The seeds of political action were already present in Francis Schaeffer's 1976 critique of *Roe v. Wade*. His words echoed a familiar phrase from the Nixon years ("silent majority") and looked forward to the "moral majority" soon to appear on the political horizon.

I believe the majority of the silent majority, young and old, will sustain the loss of liberties without raising their voices as long as their own life-styles are not threatened. And since personal peace and affluence are so often the only values that count with the majority, politicians know that to be elected they must promise these things. Politics has largely become not a matter of ideals—increasingly men and women are not stirred by the values of liberty and truth—but of supplying a constituency with a frosting of personal peace and affluence. They know that voices will not be raised as long as people have these things, or at least an illusion of them.

The clarity of this statement challenged evangelicals to think beyond their own self-interest (such as the tax-exempt status of private schools) to the most fundamental issue of all—*life*. Over time, the movement would lose that clarity, as would the scores of politicians elected with the efforts and hopes of religious activists.

Francis Schaeffer promoted *How Should We Then Live?* in 1976 with an eighteen-city book tour and a film series that was screened from coast to coast. Thousands of evangelicals were confronted with Schaeffer's blunt message of a culture in decline—and the implicit challenge to wake up and speak truth to our generation. The implicit challenge would be transformed into an explicit call for political engagement in his next two works. *Whatever Happened to the Human Race?* (1979) tackled abortion and euthanasia more directly. The evolution of Schaeffer's thought was complete with *A Christian Manifesto* (1981), in which he asserted that "a high view of Scripture and a high view of life go hand-in-hand. You cannot be faithful to what the Bible teaches about the value of human life and be in favor of abortion." Schaeffer issued a direct call to political action—but also a controversial warning. If change could not be brought about under a conservative president like Reagan, Schaeffer wrote, then Christians might have to resort to civil disobedience in defense of life.

RELABELING LIFE

What has the Religious Right achieved in its defense of life? Abortion remains the law of the land. *Roe v. Wade* continues to frame the debate and the legal parameters of abortion in America. Conservatives have been successful, however, in chipping away at the legal superstructure built on the cracked foundation of *Roe v. Wade*. Most of these victories have come in state legislatures, over forty of which have enacted parental notification laws. Conservatives have also been successful in restricting the federal funding of abortions, though the Hyde Amendment (1976)—arguably the most significant federal legislation on abortion—came three years before the Moral Majority started lobbying. A significant victory came more recently at the federal level when the Partial-Birth Abortion Ban Act was signed into law in 2003 and upheld by the Supreme Court in 2006. The record is mixed. The handful of legislative victories must be balanced against our one great achievement: If not for a vocal and active pro-life movement during the past generation, America might well be closer to current European policies on life and death. We're trending that direction—but evangelicals have probably slowed the process.

This mixed legacy has led conservative Christians to reassess whether abortion should remain the issue that defines the evangelical role in politics. The electoral potency of the issue has begun to wane, and the GOP platform has watered down its pro-life language. Tired of the old abortion wars, the public seems receptive to the attempt to shift the argument from "When does life begin?" to "What quality of life will this child enjoy?" Adoption is becoming a substitute issue for some evangelicals.

For Christians determined to live out their faith in practical ways, adoption is seen as a concrete way to demonstrate a pro-life commitment. Adoption is a beautiful thing—a picture of our adoption into the family of God—but it should never blunt our condemnation of abortion.

Another response has been to redefine the terms altogether. The phrase "culture of life," coined by Pope John Paul II in 1995, has gained currency in American politics. It hasn't taken long for politicians to figure out how much political cover the phrase provides for those who want to espouse family values on the campaign trail but don't want to work very hard to achieve them in Washington. "Culture of life" has come to refer to policies that discourage abortion and encourage adoption, an emphasis on quality-of-life issues, and even (for some) the inclusion of health care policy and environmental issues. Democratic politicians, too, have warmed up to the phrase, which suggests that a squishy middle ground is emerging in the abortion debate. For the candidate or private citizen reluctant to choose sides, the "culture of life" tactic allows one to evade the central question: "Does life begin at conception?" One can feel good about affirming life even though thousands of lives that God created are terminated each year and precious children like Marci are denied the chance to laugh and play, stroke the fur of a big brown dog or surprise their neighbors on lazy afternoons.

Another relabeling project that has gained some traction is the phrase "consistent pro-life ethic"—another phrase that has its origins (like "culture of life") in Catholic thought. The word *consistent* is important here, as it recalls Schaeffer's denunciation of evangelical hypocrisy. At first glance, there seems to be little one could object to in this expansion of the pro-life ethic. The closer you look, however, the clearer it becomes that abortion is being folded into a broader package of issues and the abortion issue is denied any special treatment. Here's how evangelical author and scholar David Gushee describes his understanding of the sanctity of life:

> Every life means every life, without exception. That includes two-month-along developing human beings in the womb, poor babies in Bangladesh, impoverished children in ghettos, abused wives and children, civilians in war zones, wounded soldiers at Walter Reed, imprisoned detainees in the war on terror, aging people living in nursing homes, mentally handicapped people, people convicted of heinous crimes. Everyone.

Linking the rights of the unborn to the rights of "people convicted of heinous crimes" is an odd way, I believe, to affirm one's commitment to life. Gushee goes on to itemize what a pro-life ethic leads him to oppose: abortion, euthanasia, war, murder, poverty, abuse, lack of adequate health care, torture, cruelty, degradation, and the death penalty. His expansive view of "pro-human wholeness" leads him to place the following policy statements under the broad rubric of life:

> I support loving and nurturing family life, racial reconciliation, restorative justice, gender equity and quality education for everyone. I support the life of culture and the mind, beauty and the arts, science and technological advancement in the service of human well-being. I oppose structures and behaviors that discriminate improperly between groups of people, block their access to these essentials of human flourishing, and therefore limit the fulfillment of their God-given potential.

Thus defined, the pro-life ethic is really one step shy of a humanistic manifesto. The orientation has shifted from God's glory to "the service of human well-being" and "human flourishing." In a life shaped so completely by man, how much room can be left for the glory of God?

It's certainly right to emphasize, as Jesus does, that we are called to a comprehensive view of life, a holistic "pro-life ethic" that extends far beyond the abortion issue. But one senses another agenda at work, one that seeks to blunt the issue, to minimize the controversy behind this most controversial of issues, to conceal one's pro-life position behind a screen of progressive causes. The phrases "culture of life" and "pro-life ethic" contain a lot of truth. But behind this soft pro-life position is a shift in values, the replotting of life as just another policy position like health care.

Still others have sought to identify "common ground" between the pro-life and pro-choice positions. Unlike the other relabeling projects, this one did not originate in Catholic seminaries or the Vatican but on the front lines of the abortion conflict in America. In the aftermath of vigorous antiabortion protests in Buffalo, New York, in 1992, area churches convened a one-day conference to discuss nonviolent protests. From these discussions emerged the Common Ground Network for Life and Choice—a structured forum that provides an opportunity for abortion opponents to practice conflict resolution in pursuit of common goals:

☆ assisting crack-addicted pregnant women
☆ preventing unwanted pregnancies
☆ providing women support during pregnancy
☆ teaching abstinence to teenagers
☆ reducing infant mortality
☆ financing school breakfast programs

This approach has caught the attention of Democratic politicians in particular, who are looking for ways to peel away some of the "values voters" that traditionally move toward the Republican party. In January 2005, long before her campaign for president officially began, Senator Hillary Clinton spoke to a pro-choice crowd in Washington DC and specifically endorsed the terminology. But the very phrase *common ground* is a cruel lie—a kind of Solomonic compromise (without the wisdom) that ends up costing a child his life.

THE PRIMACY OF LIFE

The righteousness of the pro-life position—what Schaeffer asked us many years ago to see clearly—has been compromised. And this has happened not just through artful redefinitions of the terms but also by crass political calculation. The savvy political engineering of the Christian Coalition in the 1990s did much to put a cynical spin on what religious conservatives back in the Moral Majority days held as sacrosanct. Life for the Christian Coalition became one more political issue to be balanced against other, more practical interests like winning elections. It's ironic that the architect behind this strategy, Ralph Reed, lost his own election in 2006 in large measure because of the compromises he had endorsed. His campaign was sunk by one revelation after another that demonstrated a close connection between Reed and disgraced Washington lobbyist Jack Abramoff.

One revelation that came late in the campaign—involving of all things some remote islands in the Pacific—seemed to cut straight to the hypocrisy. Seven years before the campaign, Reed's consulting firm had sent out a letter to evangelical Christians in Alabama, asking them to pressure their congressman to oppose new federal legislation concerning the Northern Mariana Islands, a U.S. commonwealth in the Pacific. Workers from Asian countries were being brought into the Marianas to work low-wage jobs producing clothes with the coveted "Made in the

U.S.A." label. Abramoff represented the Mariana commonwealth in its opposition to this legislation, which would have brought the islands into conformity with U.S. federal wage and worker safety laws. Abramoff turned again to his old friend Ralph Reed as he had done with the Indian gambling casinos.

The Reed letter declared that "the radical left, the Big Labor Union Bosses, and Bill Clinton want to pass a law preventing Chinese from coming to work on the Mariana Islands," where many "are exposed to the teachings of Jesus Christ" while working there and "are converted to the Christian faith and return to China with Bibles in their hand." Keeping the islands open to cheap imported labor was thus directly linked to the cause of Christ. The simple language of the mailing distorted the issue beyond all recognition. Most folks had probably never heard of the Marianas until this letter arrived informing them, in effect, that this was a place where Bill Clinton wanted to prevent Chinese people from getting saved. But Jack Abramoff wasn't lobbying so that Chinese men and women could come to Christ. He was representing the economic interests of the government of the Mariana Islands.

There was a darker side to the controversy. A report issued by the Interior Department a year earlier had cast an entirely different light on what foreign workers were exposed to in the Marianas. Chinese women and young girls had come to the islands to work in garment factories, and many ended up in the sex tourism industry instead. Some were even subjected, allegedly, to forced abortions. Regulation of a predatory industry that devalued life is exactly what was needed in the Mariana Islands. But it seems that even life, the most sacred of all evangelical issues, had been compromised. Nobody intended this—certainly not Ralph Reed, and certainly not the Christian voters who were manipulated with such cynicism. But the compromise happened nonetheless. Can we any longer defend the primacy of the abortion issue? I believe we can—and I believe we must, on the basis of two scriptural truths.

First, though every life is valuable to God, *the bringing forth of new life is a uniquely hallowed expression of God's work in creation and re-creation.* Jesus made the link very clearly when He told Nicodemus that he must be born again. Nicodemus was incredulous. "How can a man be born when he is old? Can he enter a second time into his mother's womb and be born?" Jesus answered by justifying this striking analogy between physical and spiritual birth.

> Do not marvel that I said to you, "You must be born again." The wind blows where it wishes, and you hear the sound of it, but cannot tell where it comes from and where it goes. So is everyone who is born of the Spirit.   JOHN 3:7-8

Jesus was saying, "Don't be surprised that I've connected spiritual birth with physical birth." The one birth mirrors the other. Both are mysteries that the human mind can never fathom. Both, too, are works of the Holy Spirit, moving over creation (see Genesis 1:2) and regenerating the human heart through justification (see Titus 3:5-7). God's sovereignty is uniquely on display in both our physical creation and our spiritual re-creation in Christ.

Second, *the story of God's work, like life itself, begins with conception.* God's work through Israel began with the promise of a child to Abraham: "Behold, Sarah your wife shall have a son" (Genesis 18:10). God's deliverance of Israel from captivity in Egypt began when a defenseless infant named Moses was set afloat among the bulrushes and was rescued from certain destruction (see Exodus 2:1-10). God's deliverance of Israel under Samson began with the promise of new life to a faithful woman in the field: "You shall conceive and bear a son" (Judges 13:3). God's work through Samuel began with the promise that Hannah would bear a son (see 1 Samuel 1). While Samuel was still in her womb, Hannah dedicated him to God. Jeremiah was called as a prophet while he was yet unborn: "Before I formed you in the womb," God said to him, "I knew you; before you were born I sanctified you; I ordained you a prophet to the nations" (Jeremiah 1:5). The unborn John the Baptist, the last of the prophets, leaped for joy in Elizabeth's womb when Mary came to visit (see Luke 1:41-44). All these examples merely look ahead to the greatest biblical endorsement of the sanctity of unborn life, when Gabriel announced to Mary that the Holy Spirit would come upon her and she would bear a son (see Luke 1:28-35). In the uniqueness of Christ's conception, we see a reminder that all life is of God—the One who moves over His creation and who brings new life into deadened hearts.

THE NEXT BATTLEGROUNDS

Abortion is the critical battleground in a much broader attack on life. If we cannot think clearly—and biblically—about the unborn, then we are ill prepared to defend life in any other context. Francis Schaeffer was right when he linked abortion to other violations of the sanctity of life, such as infanticide, physician-assisted suicide, and euthanasia. Already in 1976 he saw the inevitability of the trend line, and we're witnessing the fulfillment of that today in Western Europe and, to a lesser extent, the United States. In Holland, for example, the country that gave us Corrie ten Boom, disabled newborns have been euthanized routinely for the past two decades. Recently, the practice has been brought into public view, but there has been little if any outrage, little soul searching, and little sense of the terrible irony that this is happening in a nation that resisted the Nazis with such courage. For the Dutch today, as for the Nazis back then, the state has the power to take an innocent and defenseless human life; and the justification for terminating that life is embedded deep within the bureaucratic machinery of society. The arguments are purely material—costs and benefits to a society that confers the right to personhood on some of its citizens but denies it to others.

So far, in the United States we're only *talking* about infanticide. But that's terrifying enough. At Princeton University, the institution that gave us B. B. Warfield and John Gresham Machen and other pillars of modern evangelicalism, ethicist Peter Singer has achieved notoriety for his views that it is ethical—and socially desirable—to euthanize disabled infants. From the platform of this historically Christian university, Professor Singer argues that infants do not enter this world as persons; rather, they acquire personhood through "social construction." As such, infants have no rights, nor do they even acquire rights until society has conferred them by consensus. What the state gives, the state can take away.

In Germany, the nation that gave us Martin Luther, government authorities have been puzzled over how to address an epidemic of infant murders. Women have discarded their unwanted newborns—throwing them from balconies, strangling them, wrapping them in grocery bags and then tossing them away with the garbage. Other newborns have been found in freezers and ponds. In some cities, the medieval practice of "baby drops" has been revived so that distraught mothers have the option of abandoning their infants to the care of the state rather than hurling them to their deaths from apartment windows.

MIT researcher Steven Pinker has offered a Darwinian explanation for modern infanticide. What we're witnessing, he argues, is something perfectly normal in our species—nothing more than a primal reversal to an earlier evolutionary instinct. Lower animals do this too, so we shouldn't be terribly perplexed (he rationalizes) if a woman here or there tosses her child from the balcony. Of course, society should seek to restrain and redirect these dark impulses, but only with the understanding, Pinker argues, that this is not a moral problem we face but rather a curious biological throwback. Even our ethical consciousness—the ability to discuss and debate the rightness or wrongness of infanticide—has evolved. To an evolutionist, this "fact" alone makes us the masters of our destiny. If infanticide is "wrong," it is wrong only because we say so. Pinker has given us the ultimate materialistic explanation. The academic answer is clinical and efficient, stripped of any moral content or consideration. Women kill their children because this instinct is written into our genes. Significantly, Pinker's explanation is no different from the bureaucratic justifications that reduce people to material commodities. In both cases the element of personal responsibility is denied. The authority to take innocent human life is embedded in our genes, or deep in the empty bureaucratic soul of the modern Western state. Take your pick.

Physician-assisted suicide, too, has grown in public acceptance as the materialistic view of life has gained traction. Post-Christian Europe is once again leading the way into this dark future. It was reported in 2007, for example, that a sixty-seven-year-old German woman with fake medical papers came to the Swiss clinic Dignitas in order to die. The papers in her hand claimed that she was already dying of cirrhosis of the liver. With little further inquiry, the doctors—operating under the sanction of Swiss law—prepared a cocktail of drugs for the woman to drink. She drank the potion and died. It came to light after her death, however, that she was not suffering from a terminal illness at all. She was suffering from alcoholism and depression and had faked her papers so that she could take advantage of Switzerland's legally sanctioned "suicide clinics." A growing number of foreigners, many of them British subjects, now travel to Switzerland to end their lives in a ghoulish practice known as "death tourism."

Most Americans are still appalled, at least in the abstract, when confronted by the issue. But this, too, is changing. Physician-assisted suicide will become an unavoidable controversy as the financial pressures of health care costs continue to be tabulated. Oregon's Death with Dignity Act (1997) is the first step in that direction. Physician-assisted suicide will lead inevitably to euthanasia, and this issue, in the years ahead, will almost certainly become one of the great battlefields in the struggle for life.

If one has adopted a materialistic worldview, then infanticide, suicide, and euthanasia make perfectly good sense under the right circumstances. But they make no sense at all to one whose world begins and ends with the sovereignty of God. If we believe that God is all knowing and all powerful, but also good, then what sanction can there be for a practice that rejects each of these divine attributes?

Our positions on the great controversies of our day should not be determined by a voting guide or the policy positions of conservative think tanks; they should be determined by the character and nature of God. Scripture refutes the false compassion of suicide and euthanasia with the true compassion of a loving God. He is a "God of all comfort, who comforts us in all our tribulation, that we may be able to comfort those who are in any trouble, with the comfort with which we ourselves are comforted by God" (2 Corinthians 1:3-4). One of the most radical ideas of the Christian faith is that the same God who has revealed Himself in creation, in Scripture, and in His Son, Jesus Christ, is a good God who desires good things for His fallen creation. His thoughts toward us are "of peace and not of evil," to give us "a future and a hope" (Jeremiah 29:11). This is a radical idea precisely because it challenges the entrenched doubting of our human nature. Sin originated in the question that Adam and Eve lodged against the essential character of their Creator. Every form of sin since the Garden of Eden, including the false compassion of doc-tor-assisted suicide, is a repudiation of God's goodness.

When Job lost everything and sat in ashes, his body covered in boils, his wife spoke to him with the voice of Satan. "Do you still hold fast to your integrity?" she sneered. "Curse God and die!" Job's wife was ques-tioning—with finality—the goodness of God. How could a good God allow this evil to come upon a righteous man? Those who justify taking a life out of compassion are denying, as Job's wife did, the goodness and sovereignty of God. For the Christian, living is more than the fulfillment of *my* interests and desires. If I was created to know God, then the quality-of-life argument is essentially taken off the table. Paul's prayer was "that I may know Him and the power of His resurrection, and the fellowship of His sufferings" (Philippians 3:10). In the midst of a life that, humanly speaking, had taken a severe downward slide on the quality scale, Paul affirmed that the ultimate purpose of living is to know God intimately.

Later on in the narrative about Job, in the depths of his suffering, he affirmed that "my Redeemer lives" (Job 19:25). In the darkest hour of Job's life, God granted him one of the most glorious glimpses into the hope of the Resurrection, a hope that was foreshadowed by what would happen to Job himself. God restored his family and his health to him in a beautiful picture of what will happen to each one of us. If we live long enough, each of us will see our loved ones grow old, grow weak, perhaps even suffer long illnesses, and then eventually die. We can expect the same for ourselves. It is the common legacy of our fallen world. But we see in the story of Job the promise of resurrection life. We see the goodness of God shining through the darkest hours of human suffering.

The defenders of suicide and euthanasia may try to put a loving, compassionate face on the termination of life, but the example of Job in Scripture suggests that euthanasia is nothing less than cursing God—that is, rejecting His goodness and sovereignty over life. As our world embraces a materialistic definition of human life, we must answer the ancient call of Scripture to be a people who hold with clarity the view that our days are numbered by our Creator. A people who hold with certainty the view that God, in His goodness, allows suffering to perfect His good work in our lives. A people who hold with faith the promise of the Resurrection and the eternal enjoyment of God.

THEREFORE, CHOOSE LIFE

Fund-raising banquets are not usually known for their great cuisine, but the chicken with white sauce was quite good. My wife and I had been asked to join our pastor and his wife in representing our church at the dinner. The Blue Ridge Pregnancy Center was introducing its new director and securing annual pledges for its upcoming projects.

"Why don't you just lick it clean?" my wife said, pointing to my empty plate. But there wasn't any need to, since a really incredible strawberry cream dessert was waiting.

I looked around the banquet hall at three hundred men and women, young and old, black and white. The irreducible and nonnegotiable value of life had brought us together—the belief that life, of all things, was worth defending. Nobody here was interested in compromise. We weren't talking about a culture of life or a pro-life ethic. Nobody was looking for common ground between "life" and "choice."

We moved our chairs around to face the podium, where Lori Meetre had been introduced and was beginning her talk. I was expecting a strictly business presentation from the center's new director, but it was clear from her opening words that this would be deeply personal. "Twenty-five years ago my life changed forever." The room was hushed as Lori took us back to her high school years when, as a new believer, she wrote a paper in her

English class on abortion. The paper stated categorically that "abortion is wrong because abortion is murder."

When the graded papers were returned, Lori's teacher wanted to speak with her after class. "Have you considered the fact that you've never been in that situation? How can you say what you would or would not do?"

But Lori was adamant. "I could never do this," she repeated, "because abortion is murder."

Of course, we knew where the story was going, but that didn't lessen the intensity of what Lori went on to relate. Within two years, she was a freshman in college—and she was pregnant. Suddenly, abortion seemed the easy solution for a "problem" that threatened to change everything in her life. Sitting in the clinic and waiting for her name to be called, Lori didn't realize that abortion was just as life-changing as pregnancy.

We heard about the nightmares and depression, the overwhelming sense of loss and guilt that followed the *procedure*, as it's called. Abortion exacts a high emotional toll—one that's seldom advertised by those who advocate "a woman's right to choose." Some pro-choice groups have quietly admitted this and begun offering counseling services to their postabortion clients. One Oakland-based nonprofit group, Exhale, even offers postabortion e-cards that family and friends can send to a loved one recovering from an abortion. We could expect this from an organization that lists among its core values the belief that "abortion can be a normal part of the reproductive lives of women and girls." The attempt to normalize the destruction of life is the central strategy of those who view abortion as a choice, the end result of a cost-benefit analysis.

Lori went on to describe another approach to the trauma of abortion. It's an approach that also recognizes the grief and sense of loss but refuses to normalize the sin itself. Lori spoke of healing and forgiveness. She gave witness to the grace of God. And then she explained how the battle for life is waged at Blue Ridge Pregnancy Center. Volunteers mentor and disciple not only the young women but the young men as well. With sensitivity and love, they work hard to meet the physical, material, emotional, and spiritual needs of their clients. Some come to the clinic and choose life even though they have previously terminated an earlier pregnancy. Counseling and small-group Bible studies are available to help women as they overcome the lingering effects of the choices they have made in the past. This clinic—like clinics all around the country—ministers to the whole person with the love and forgiveness of Jesus Christ.

As I sat at the table with my empty plate in front of me, I realized that Lori had presented the real face of the pro-life movement. Not hate-filled radicals with pipe bombs. Not men in dark suits with big black Bibles, but people who identify with sinners because we are *all* sinners. Men and women who say with Paul, "*We ourselves were also once foolish, disobedient, deceived, serving various lusts and pleasures, living in malice and envy, hateful and hating one another*" (Titus 3:3, emphasis added). We are the kind of men and women Paul described in 1 Corinthians 6:11 after itemizing every known sin in the ancient world as a buildup to these stunning words: "And such were some of you." The testimony that can begin this way is the testimony that impacts lives and draws men and women to Jesus Christ.

Lori ended by quoting Deuteronomy 30:19, where Moses delivered a stark choice to the children of Israel as they stood on the threshold of the Jordan River.

> I call heaven and earth as witnesses today against you, that I have set before you life and death, blessing and cursing; therefore choose life, that both you and your descendants may live.

Behind us is the wilderness. Before us lies a land flowing with milk and honey. How are we going to live in the land? How are we going to experience the fullness of God's blessings? We should be people who choose life. And we should be people who help others choose life as well.

☆

Francis Schaeffer's haunting question—*How should we then live?*—was initially posed against the broad sweep of Western culture, a story many centuries in the making. Though Schaeffer was looking at long historical trends, his question spoke to a generation of evangelicals, giving form, direction, and immediacy to the movement once called the New Right. Evangelicals have drifted from that initial clarity of purpose. Schaeffer's question remains on the table. What should our response be? It might sound too simplistic to say, but the only answer Scripture gives is that we should live for Christ. Neither a cop-out nor a forfeiture of our civic responsibilities, living for Christ is a biblical mandate. Nor is this just another way of saying "pro-life ethic." The biblical approach does assume a comprehensive view of life, but it rejects the idea that life must be plotted on a political landscape. This is not to deny that real political decisions will flow from our beliefs, but our beliefs are not validated by political action. The biblical approach refuses to translate life into a political platform on health care or the environment. Good Christians can disagree about these issues, but there can be no disagreement about the sanctity of life.

These two sides of the equation—*life* and *living*—must go hand in hand for the Christian, as they did for the early church and as they do for volunteers in clinics all across the nation—like the Blue Ridge Pregnancy Center or the Liberty Godparent Home founded by Jerry Falwell. The church fathers vigorously opposed the degradation of life in Roman society. They were outspoken in their opposition to abortion, infanticide, and the gladiatorial blood sports. But the early Christians were also known for the concrete steps they took to realize their values in the larger community. If life is the prime value, then it should be reflected not just in the candidates we vote for or the public policies we embrace but in the way we treat our neighbors and defend the weak. As we model the humility of Christ in sacrifice and service to others, we demonstrate that Kingdom living rejects the worldly values of power and self-interest. In so living, we refute the barren materialism that would reduce all life to biological and chemical forces. In so living, we demonstrate the high price tag that our Creator placed on human life—a price tag that reads, "Redeemed . . . with the precious blood of Jesus Christ" (1 Peter 1:18-19).

Why is life such a big deal? Because we were created to know God and be known by Him. Because life—in all its beauty and mystery—makes possible the eternal enjoyment of God.

CHAPTER SEVEN

A Simple Call to Virtue

The Sermon on the Mount is probably the best-known part of the teaching of Jesus, though arguably it is the least understood, and certainly it is the least obeyed. It is the nearest thing to a manifesto that he ever uttered, for it is his own description of what he wanted his followers to be and to do.

— **JOHN R. W. STOTT**

Growing up in a fundamentalist church, I heard a lot of Sunday morning sermons on the third chapter of John. But as I sat in the pew with my Scofield Reference Bible open on my lap, I heard very little teaching from the Sermon on the Mount. It's a familiar section of Scripture, but conservative Christians seem ill at ease with the most concentrated teaching Jesus gave in His earthly ministry. Could it be that we're slightly uncomfortable with the sharp denunciations of wealth and power, unsure how to square this with our political and economic values? It doesn't help, of course, that liberals love to quote the Sermon, especially the part about judging. We struggle to understand what Jesus taught about living in the Kingdom of God, and so we cherry-pick what we like and relegate what we don't to some future millennial age.

Our ambivalence toward the Sermon on the Mount can be traced back a hundred years to the Fundamentalist-Modernist Controversy that split the Presbyterian church. In the pivotal fifty years that followed the Civil War, the church in America was falling under the sway of "scientific" historical methods and a liberal theology usually associated with German universities abroad. Americans who studied theology in Berlin, Heidelberg, Leipzig, and Bonn assimilated these new ideas and brought them home. As modernism invaded the American church, new movements such as fundamentalism would emerge, new methods of biblical interpretation such as a dispensationalism would be developed, and even a new Bible—the Scofield Reference Bible—would be published.

Modernist biblical methods, especially the so-called higher criticism, undermined the authority of Scripture and paved the way for the Darwinian worldview to take full root in the West. The Bible was approached as a philological specimen to be studied, not the supernaturally revealed Word of God to be obeyed. What the ignorant Christian in the pew called the Holy Scripture was reclassified by the scholarly elite as a tissue of oral myths and legends that had accumulated into a written text. The higher critics would dissect a given passage, highlight the strands of "mythology" that underlie this story or that, identify the cultural reasons why scribes would have rewritten and combined these stories, and thereby reconstruct the development of the biblical texts over time. The Bible was thus repackaged as a material product—the end result of historical conditions, not divine revelation.

Once the Bible had been stripped of its authority, what remained for Christians to believe? Liberal theologians certainly recognized Jesus as a great teacher, and the Sermon on the Mount was held up as a noble and profound statement of the ethical life. But that was pretty much it.

In the late nineteenth century, conservative Christians were understandably troubled by this materialistic approach to Scripture. But it was not enough to reject modernism and simply restate the orthodox doctrines of inspiration and inerrancy. Bible-believing Christians knew intuitively that they would still have to account for the historical processes that higher criticism had exposed. They would still have to explain the apparent anomalies in the text, the different ways God was portrayed from Genesis to Revelation, the different covenants that God had established with humanity. These were historical, chronological problems. Either the Bible really did evolve over time as the critics claimed, or there was a divine purpose behind all this diversity in Scripture.

The solution was found in dispensationalism. Where modernism found a historical *progression* in the text, conservatives saw instead a *progressive* revelation. God had revealed Himself in Scripture through the establishment of unique covenants with Adam, Noah, Abraham, Israel, and David. The revelation of God continued in the ministry of Christ and into the church age. Looking into the future, God would culminate His work in history in the millennial reign of Christ. The higher critics had viewed Scripture through a historical lens as a text that had developed through the *periods* of Near Eastern civilization; fundamentalists answered this by *periodizing* God's work from Creation to Judgment. Dispensationalism was thus a vigorous response to the methods of higher criticism, as James Sawyer has noted:

> These issues of development and change in the Scriptures which gave birth to dispensationalism were the same issues which engaged higher criticism in the nineteenth century. In many respects dispensationalism represents the mirror opposite of higher criticism, confronting the same issues but solving them on totally different bases.

On one level, dispensationalism makes a lot of sense. It's a convenient way to harmonize the unique covenants God established with His people. It certainly articulates how the old covenant, with its typological symbolism, and the new covenant, with its fulfillments in Christ, fit together into a unified whole. That's why orthodox Christianity has always accepted a modified form of dispensational interpretation, even if it only acquired the specific label in the late nineteenth century. But turned into an interpretative grid, ultra-dispensationalism can obscure the fact that a consistent God lies behind the whole sweep of Scripture. From beginning to end, He is a God of holiness, mercy, love, and forgiveness. A God who demands obedience and worship. A God who cannot lie, who is faithful to what He has promised. And as with all interpretive systems (Calvinism is another example), the danger lies in pressing Scripture through the fine filter of our own devices. Our man-made systems of interpretation can work too well sometimes. They can explain away the complexities of Scripture to such an extent that we no longer hear what God is saying to us.

Unfortunately, that's what happened to the Sermon on the Mount.

And that's why I seldom heard any preaching from Matthew 5–7. The Bible I used as a child was just about the only study Bible that was fundamentalist-approved—the Scofield Reference Bible, an impressive synthesis of conservative scholarship that often blurred the lines between Holy Scripture and theological interpretation. Scofield's notes were almost Talmudic in their authority. The pre-1967 edition that I used, the "Old Scofield Bible," even placed Bishop Ussher's chronology in the central margins of the text, telling me, for example, that Creation had occurred in 4004 BC. The notes were usually helpful, but almost always dogmatic, as when Scofield divided Scripture into "seven dispensations" and relegated the Sermon on the Mount to the future millennial reign of Christ. This "divine constitution for the righteous government of the earth"—which was Scofield's description of Matthew 5–7—"gives neither the privilege nor the duty of the Church. These are found in the Epistles."

Though Scofield also conceded that the Sermon "clearly has a beautiful moral application to the Christian," the overwhelming message

his notes conveyed (to me, anyway) was that the Sermon was an awkward portion of Scripture that I could concern myself with later—after
Christ was already reigning on earth. Charles Ryrie, himself a dispensationalist and author of another popular study Bible, tried to soften the
impact of Scofield's notes. Scofield was just being a careful interpreter,
Ryrie argued. The "dispensational interpretation of the Sermon on the
Mount simply tries to follow consistently the principle of literal, normal, or plain interpretation. It results in not trying to relegate primarily
and fully the teachings of the Sermon to the believer in this age. But it
does not in the least disregard the ethical principles of the Sermon as
being not only applicable but also binding on believers today." But for
generations of believers such as myself, the damage had already been
done. The Sermon on the Mount, I came to understand, was the favorite
passage of liberal Christians who denied the gospel and would replace it
instead with the Kingdom teachings of Jesus that weren't even intended
for the church age.

As Cyrus Ingersoll Scofield set out to publish his new reference Bible,
he found a kindred spirit in Arno Gaebelein. A German immigrant and
theologian, Gaebelein was a dispensationalist, an ardent opponent of
liberalism, and a well-connected friend of wealthy benefactors who were
eager to support Scofield's project. In his commentary on Matthew,
Gaebelein clearly shuffled the Sermon off to the future millennial age
just as Scofield had done.

> A good deal in the sermon on the mount appears mostly in con-
> nection with the earth. The meek are to inherit the earth. The
> church, however, is heavenly.... The magna charta of the church
> is in the Epistles of Paul, to whom the full revelation of the church
> was given.

This line of demarcation between the teaching of Jesus and the teaching of Paul was here mandated by a rigid dispensationalism. Gaebelein argued that since the church wasn't established when Jesus sat down to teach on that Galilean hill, His teaching is actually less authoritative for the church than the epistles of Paul. Ironically, the theological liberals that Scofield and Gaebelein were so passionate in refuting also argued for an interpretive fire wall between the Gospels and the Epistles. For liberals, however, the ethical teachings of Jesus are authoritative and foundational. The dispensationalists reverse the polarities and give first place instead to Paul's writings to the church.

Both approaches are wrong.

It's troubling to read Gaebelein's almost patronizing dismissal of the Beatitudes—especially "Blessed are the meek, for they shall inherit the earth." Gaebelein stated matter-of-factly that since the church is "heavenly," this certainly can't be referring to us. Maybe there's some generalized sense in which a spiritual application can be made, he conceded, but this meekness is looking ahead to the millennium. Christians in the here and now are to take our cues from the magna charta of the Christian life: the Epistles. But when we do this, and specifically when we turn to Paul's letter to the Philippians, we read the following:

> Let nothing be done through selfish ambition or conceit, but in lowliness of mind let each esteem others better than himself. Let each of you look out not only for his own interests, but also for the interests of others. **PHILIPPIANS 2:3-4**

Where did Paul find the ultimate model for his ethical teaching about meekness? "Let this mind be in you which was also in Christ Jesus" (2:5). The meekness that Jesus preached in His Sermon is the same meekness He displayed before Pilate, when "as a lamb to the slaughter, and as a sheep before its shearers is silent, so He opened not His mouth" (Isaiah 53:7).

Consider, too, Paul's message to the church elders in Ephesus. Paul reminded them that "I have not shunned to declare to you the whole counsel of God" (Acts 20:27). As we continue reading his Sermon, we learn that the "whole counsel" clearly included the words of Jesus, as Paul ended his address by saying: "Remember the words of the Lord Jesus, that He said, 'It is more blessed to give than to receive'" (Acts 20:35). These words, which convey the spirit of the Sermon on the Mount, aren't found in the Gospels at all; they were preserved as part of the oral teaching passed down in the early church. Significantly, Paul was violating Arno Gaebelein's dispensationalist guidelines. Paul even gave priority to the words of Jesus by making them the last thing he said before kneeling and praying with the elders in Ephesus. We cannot separate the teaching and ministry of Christ from the rest of the New Testament without missing the whole point of the gospel. "Be ye followers of me," Paul told the early church, "even as I also am of Christ" (1 Corinthians 11:1, KJV).

It really matters that evangelicals have been so deaf to the great Sermon Jesus preached. Ironically, as we've consigned the Sermon to the future Kingdom age, we've failed to hear Jesus warn us about our own kingdom-building in the here and now. Our casual dismissal of the Sermon on the Mount explains a lot of things that are painful to admit, such as my nationalistic and militaristic impulses *right now*, my crude addiction to prosperity and material success *right now*, and my comfort with law and religiosity *right now*. Jesus rejected the power paradigms of this world and issued instead a simple call to virtue. He challenged our political paradigms with a message of nonviolence. He challenged our economic paradigms with a message of dependence on God. He challenged our religious paradigms with a message of authenticity. We find in this great Sermon the answer for how to live with faith in a nation that denies these very values—a nation that was never under God.

REJECTING THE POLITICAL PARADIGMS

Jesus had many opportunities to lead a political crusade, but He passed up every one of them. At the outset of His ministry, Jesus was tempted in the wilderness with political power:

> The devil took Him up on an exceedingly high mountain, and
> showed Him all the kingdoms of the world and their glory. And he
> said to Him, "All these things I will give You if You will fall down
> and worship me." MATTHEW 4:8-9

Satan was offering Jesus a way to avoid the Cross. It was a political solution—immediate dominion over the fallen world that Jesus would buy back with His own blood. At the end of His ministry, too, Jesus might have opted for a quick political settlement to the world's problems. As He rode into Jerusalem, the cheering throngs greeting Him with shouts of "Hosanna," Jesus held the crowds in the palm of His hand. But instead of closing His fist and grasping the political power that was His for the taking, Jesus opened up His palms and received the nails.

It should come as no surprise, then, that Jesus delivered a withering attack on the power paradigms of this world. He had rejected those very paradigms when He humbled Himself, took flesh upon His deity, and submitted Himself to the shame of the Cross (see Philippians 2:5-8). The Beatitudes can be read as an implicit critique of the politically powerful who would oppress and exploit others. Those who "persecuted the prophets who were before you" (Matthew 5:12) felt threatened by the righteous witness to a Power greater than their own. The solution is not to entrust political power to better leaders (although this is a good and desirable thing) but to recognize that we don't look to the political system and its machinery for moral and spiritual remedies. The power paradigms of this world reward self-assertion and self-will. Kingdom living rejects those values and replaces them with self-sacrifice and self-denial.

The rejection of political power lies at the heart of Jesus' teaching on nonviolence (see Matthew 5:38-48). Sounding vaguely like a progressive value and not a conservative one, nonviolence usually doesn't rank very high on the evangelical agenda. Unfortunately, evangelicals have ceded this important Kingdom principle to those who have redefined nonviolence as a synonym for pacifism. Jesus certainly repudiated the arrogant and self-serving actions of the powerful; however, He never addressed the motivation of human governments in the waging of war and peace, but rather the motivation of human hearts toward our neighbors. This is a crucial distinction—a continental divide between evangelical and liberal theology. Liberals are wrong to misinterpret Jesus, just as evangelicals are wrong to ignore Him. Where liberals wrongly find justification for expansive government policies in the words of Jesus, evangelicals should find instead a Kingdom ethic for selfless, Spirit-empowered living.

So how are we to understand Christ's teaching on nonviolence? How can evangelicals reclaim this Christ-centered principle? Jesus' teaching is best understood as a rejection of worldly power that must have personal application. When Jesus called His disciples to be peacemakers (see Matthew 5:9), He was not issuing a position paper on foreign policy. He was teaching us a social ethic to govern our day-to-day relationships. As the Kingdom of God becomes established in our hearts, relationships will be transformed. Where we once asserted *our* rights and *our* territories, we find a new impulse—a Spirit-guided impulse—to concede and give ground to one another's interests. Sacrificial love is the flip side of violence, and it is here that we struggle most in living out Christ's ethic of peace.

We may foolishly think that violent behavior doesn't "run in our family" and thereby miss the whole point that Jesus is making. As middle-class American Christians, we may feel smug in the refinement of our legal traditions and cultural behaviors. But we may also be surprised that in the list of violent sins Paul warned the early church about, he felt obliged to mention—among the character traits that disqualify one from church leadership—the kind of bare-knuckled brawling we associate with a Hells Angels motorcycle bar. After all, most of us generally don't struggle with being a "brawler" or a "striker" (1 Timothy 3:3, KJV); we don't usually resort to fisticuffs over the backyard fence. But these admonitions are intended for us as well. Violence *does* run in our family. Embedded in our old Adamic nature are violent intentions toward those who have wronged us. Modern civil law can powerfully restrain our outward behavior, but it can never tame our hearts. "From whence come wars and fightings among you?" James asked. "Come they not hence, even of your lusts that war in your members?" (4:1, KJV). Jesus taught us in the Sermon on the Mount that we commit murder—no less than Cain did—when we hate our brother (see Matthew 5:21-22). Kingdom living always comes back to matters of the heart.

The issue gets a little thornier when we project Jesus' teaching out beyond our backyard fence into the global sphere, the remote violence "over there" that we debate in political campaigns and see through television images. Must the rejection of this world's power paradigms lead us inevitably to pacifism? Not at all. Even though pacifism is a conviction for some believers—one of those differences among Christians that should be respected—it is hard nonetheless to imagine the early Christians denouncing the Roman military and organizing protests against the

Empire's campaigns abroad. (By the same token, it's just as hard to imagine they would ever stage pro-war rallies.) Policies of pacifism or interventionism come down to personal conviction, not biblical mandate. Jesus never addressed, nor did Paul, the position Christians should take on national defense and international affairs. It is naive to say that the injunction to turn the other cheek (see Matthew 5:39) applies with equal force to nation states as it does to Kingdom believers. Those who make this connection are making the very error they attribute to the evangelical Right, namely confusing Kingdom values with this world system.

But regardless of where one stands on war and peace, there can be no disagreement about the corrosive effects of delighting in violence. The motives of our hearts do matter, as Jesus taught repeatedly in the Sermon on the Mount. I recall the run-up to the Gulf War in the 1990s and the feeling—not a godly one, to be sure—that this would be a fight worth watching. It might as well have been the Friday night fights, as CNN turned us all into eager spectators with front-row seats. I look back at this now with a sense of shame—shame at the fascination with smart bombs, the pride in military superiority, the confidence that a great evil had been righted. These attitudes, ranging from technological curiosity to "righteous anger," only served to mask a primitive bloodlust, one just slightly more sophisticated than the gladiatorial shows in ancient Rome. With flags waving and the national anthem blaring, it was hard to see this primal response clearly. Christians like myself had cloaked our basest instincts in the much more positive garb of patriotic fervor. What I now see more clearly, though, is how *the glorification of violence* can be disguised as technological wonder and *the justification of violence* as righteous anger. I had failed to reject, as my first order of business, the power paradigms of this world system.

We can love our country and be good citizens without falling into the trap of nationalism—a kind of pride that separates and classifies people in ways that God does not recognize. We should follow the example of Paul, who rejected the nationalistic impulses that once motivated him, proud impulses that spring from the old sinful nature:

> If anyone else thinks he may have confidence in the flesh, I more so: circumcised the eighth day, of the stock of Israel, of the tribe of Benjamin, a Hebrew of the Hebrews; concerning the law, a Pharisee; concerning zeal, persecuting the church; concerning the righteousness which is in the law, blameless. But what things were gain to me, these I have counted loss for Christ. **PHILIPPIANS 3:4-7**

National distinctions will mean nothing as we stand before the "sea of glass" described in the last book of the Bible. The redeemed of the Lord will one day be worshiping Christ as one family and singing one anthem: "You . . . have redeemed us to God by Your blood out of every tribe and tongue and people and nation" (Revelation 5:9).

REJECTING THE ECONOMIC PARADIGMS

Jesus is very clear, too, in His rejection of the economic power of this world system. The world idolizes the entrepreneur, the successful businessperson, the tycoon who extracts wealth from the raw material of this world. John Paul Getty, the oil baron, mocked the spirit of the Beatitudes when he said, "The meek will inherit the earth, but not its mineral rights." Jesus is not impressed, however, by our riches and our financial success. Over and over in the Sermon, we're reminded of our total dependence upon God and we're warned about the lure of worldly riches. We are to lay up treasures in heaven, not on earth (see Matthew 6:19). We cannot serve God and mammon—money (see 6:24). We shouldn't fret even about the necessities of life—food and clothing—since our Father knows how to clothe the lilies of the field (see 6:25-34).

Jesus is not rejecting hard work and frugality, stewardship and financial responsibility. He is, however, utterly rejecting the crass pursuit of prosperity and material wealth. He's rejecting the "gospel of success" that has carried so many evangelicals away with its false promises.

When we see the world's economic paradigm in its grotesque, heretical form—as an American gospel—we're able to see more clearly what's at stake for believers. The publisher of *Forbes* magazine, Rich Karlgaard, defines this gospel of success in ways that should trouble us deeply. In an essay entitled "The American Dream and the Gospel of Success," Karlgaard confesses that he had been looking for a "positive strain of Christianity" as a young man and had found that in Norman Vincent Peale. Peale "preached just what I wanted to hear, *needed* to hear, *knew* in my bones to be authentic and true," Karlgaard writes.

> Life had a purpose. Each of us was designed by God to fulfill a purpose. That purpose was not to sit around in a hair shirt and eat pickled fish and feel lousy about ourselves, as per my Lutheran upbringing. God's purpose was to go out in the world and do great things. Invent great products. Build great companies. Inspire employees. Thrill customers. These were great and noble things.

Karlgaard goes on to praise two Depression-era tracts that preach the American Dream—Napoleon Hill's *Think and Grow Rich* and Dale Carnegie's *How to Win Friends and Influence People*, both published in 1937. "Let the skeptics scoff," Karlgaard writes. "The American gospel of success has given millions like me their first vivid picture of the American dream."

The great fallacy behind Karlgaard's "good news" about the American Dream is that it rests on an unbiblical view of humanity. Yes, as Karlgaard states, life does have a purpose. But it's not to invent new gadgets and thrill new customers. It's to glorify God. Once again, everything in the Sermon on the Mount comes down to the motives of the heart. Jesus does not condemn prosperity. He does not condemn the invention of gadgets and the thrilling of customers. Instead, He condemns the pursuit of *wealth* whenever it becomes a substitute for the pursuit of *God*. The so-called rich young ruler who wanted to follow Christ ended up walking away when Jesus told him to sell all he had and give to the poor (see Mark 10:17-22). What Jesus said to him cut straight through the young man's wealth to the idolatry of his heart.

Once again, there's a flip side to this. The greatest check we could place on our selfish hearts is to substitute generosity for personal gain. Cardinal Ratzinger, who would later become Pope Benedict XVI, warned that Western culture was falling under "a dictatorship of relativism which does not recognize anything for certain and which has as its highest goal *one's own ego and one's own desires.*" The true gospel has always called men and women to live outside themselves, to live for something greater than their own narrow interests. The Christian does not measure generosity only in material ways, as determined by how big our tax deduction is for charitable contributions. Rather, we are to be generous of spirit too, by dispensing forgiveness and grace—even when there is no material benefit to be gained.

REJECTING THE RELIGIOUS PARADIGMS

Jesus reserved His harshest criticism for the Pharisees, whose hypocrisy He exposed with ruthless candor. Corrupted as they were by the political and economic paradigms of power, the Pharisees had turned the sacred things of God into the carnal indulgence of self. The world's religious paradigm always starts with a privileged class of *knowers*, be they priests or sages or clergymen or monks. These are the guardians of the law, the interpreters of sacred texts, the custodians of the holy places. Every religion has them, and Christianity is no exception. The medieval Catholicism that Luther challenged was a hierarchy of privileged knowledge. The contents of the Bible were a closely guarded secret, written in a priestly language that the common people couldn't understand. In time, Protestant seminaries, which grew out of Luther's challenge to Rome's stranglehold on truth, also reverted to the same paradigm, in which knowledge is power.

Paul understood the world's religious paradigm well. As a Pharisee zealous for the law (see Philippians 3:5-6), he had used his specialized education as a weapon against the early church. Paul did not repudiate knowledge when he came to Christ. Instead, the Holy Spirit illuminated his vast knowledge of the Old Testament and equipped him uniquely for that great task of theological synthesis—the book of Romans. Paul's experience was unique, but he recognized that the mysteries of God were available for free download by ordinary Christians like you and me. Paul prayed that we would attain "to all riches of the full assurance of understanding, to the knowledge of the mystery of God, both of the Father and of Christ, in whom are hidden all the treasures of wisdom and knowledge" (Colossians 2:2-3).

Paul always envisioned that a healthy church would see the knowledge gap close between shepherds and sheep. The letters he wrote were to be read and taught in all the churches—not chained to the pulpit under lock and key. Those entrusted with the mysteries of God have a divine responsibility not to hoard these riches but to dispense them freely. In so doing, the world's religious paradigm is rejected. But in order for this to happen, shepherds must have a heart for service, not job security, and sheep must have hearts that hunger after God, not ears itching for the gospel of success.

The sincerity of the heart before God is the great underlying theme of the Sermon on the Mount. If we fail to recognize this, we will misinterpret and misapply everything Jesus taught. It's not *politics* that Jesus rejected, but the pursuit of power. It's not *prosperity* that's wrong, but the pursuit of riches. It's not *knowledge* that Jesus abhorred, but legalism and hypocrisy. Here's the problem though: The one often leads to the other. Power, wealth, and knowledge are intoxicating. Political power makes us self-important. Economic power makes us self-sufficient. Religious power makes us self-righteous.

Ultimately, this great theme—the sincere, humble, and obedient heart of worship before God—validates the Sermon's message for us today. We struggle constantly with the motives of our hearts, even when doing good. We need to be confronted with the stark message of two kingdoms, two ethics, two paradigms. Sure, it's difficult to live out the teaching that Jesus gave us. It's difficult because it violates every default setting of our human nature. But we would be wrong to reject this Kingdom ethic merely because it's difficult. Paul admitted that he, too, struggled with doing right and avoiding wrong (see Romans 7:15). But Paul never concluded from this that he should stop pursuing righteousness. Paul's answer was for us to live through the indwelling power of Jesus Christ, not the power of our flesh (see Galatians 2:20). As we die to self, the fruit of the Spirit will abound in our lives. The world's power paradigms feed our flesh, which is why it's so difficult, as Jesus said, for a rich man to enter the Kingdom of God or for a respected Pharisee like Nicodemus to be born again.

This struggle of the heart answers with finality the curious objection Arno Gaebelein has raised to those, like myself, who see the Sermon as a manifesto for Christian living: "People attempt to make the sermon on the mount the standard of their lives," Gaebelein wrote. "They apply it to

themselves in the least details and get into legal bondage. The flesh given
so much to legality likes this only too well." Gaebelein never clarifies why
the Sermon should not apply directly to my life *right now* just because
some people have distorted its message. Hasn't he merely restated the
central problem that Jesus was addressing? People who turn the Sermon
into legal bondage have misunderstood Jesus in the most basic way. They
have taken His denunciation of dead religious ritual and turned it into
another form of dead religious ritual. But if we listen, really listen, to what
Jesus is telling us about our hearts, our priorities, our allegiances, we will
find it impossible to go on living the same way. We will be forced to reject
the world's power paradigms and conform ourselves instead to God's way
of doing things in the world.

HOW GOD DOES THINGS

We like to think big, dream big, plan big. God does too. But He always
starts small. God starts with individuals—faithful men and women—
before moving on to families, then communities, and finally the world.
Too often we have reversed God's pattern of doing business. We want
to change the world first, as though we can get the quickest return on
our investment by wrestling the world's political machinery into God's
corner. But God takes a ground-up approach when it comes to changing
the world. The life of Abraham, the man of faith, illustrates the fact that
God's work always starts in the regenerated hearts of individuals who
have been called out of the nations to be witnesses to the truth. When
God called Abram, He gave him a promise and a new name. Obedience
to God meant turning his back on the easy, comfortable acceptance of
the affluent Mesopotamian culture he knew. Obedience meant looking
"for a city which hath foundations, whose builder and maker is God"

(Hebrews 11:10, KJV). Obedience meant living with faith in a culture that was definitely not under God.

God continues His work in families. What was God's promise to Abraham? That he would be the father of a great family—a patriarchal line that would issue from his loins. All through Scripture we see God working through godly families to raise up His servants in a godless age. The judges Samuel and Samson were raised by godly parents. King David came from the family line of Ruth and Boaz. And in the ultimate endorsement of families, God brought His Son into the godly home of Joseph and Mary.

Godly families are then the foundation for godly communities that bear witness to the truth. It was not just a family that God promised to Abraham but a nation—a God-fearing community within the world. In living out the law of God entrusted to this community, the children of Israel were to be living examples of the holiness of God. We, too, as a "royal priesthood" and a "peculiar people" (1 Peter 2:9, KJV) "among whom [we] shine as lights in the world" (Philippians 2:15), are to be a faith community that points people away from ourselves, away from our parochial interests, and toward the holiness of our Creator. There is no higher calling.

God's work in the world comes last, and it always rests upon the foundation of His work in individuals, families, and communities of believers. The end result of God's promise to Abraham is that "all the nations of the earth" would be blessed through him. This prophecy was fulfilled through Jesus Christ, born from the line of Abraham. We who were "far off," as Paul wrote to the Ephesians, "have been brought near by the blood of Christ" (2:13). The middle wall of partition has been broken down, and we have been adopted by faith into Abraham's spiritual family (see Galatians 3:29). Jesus is the fulfillment of God's promise to Abraham, but He also illustrates the same pattern of how God works in the world. Jesus came into an earthly family, and He trained a community of followers, His disciples, to take the Good News to the ends of the earth.

If this is how God works, then I have a responsibility to get my own house in order before turning my attention to the world. I must allow God's work to begin in *my* life first. I must bend my will to His; I must sift my worldly allegiances through the filter of Scripture and bring every thought captive to Christ. And then I must be the kind of husband and father that God requires of me. In a world that values power and control, a world that promotes material success and career advancement, I must exhibit the servanthood of Christ in my most intimate relationships. I must also live within my community as a good citizen—one who honors the king and submits to the powers that are ordained of God. Certainly, I must defend what is moral and just; I must identify myself, even as the early Christians did, with the nonnegotiable values of life and truth. I should be a good steward of my vote and exercise that right of citizenship as God gives me wisdom. But I should always do this with humility, knowing that I represent God to the world. My life and my words should declare the Christian message of hope—a message that takes us beyond the ebb and flow of the historical moment to the unfolding of God's eternal purpose. People have little hope for their own individual lives today, and they have even less hope for the future. In a darkening post-Christian world where people fear terrorism, global warming, and nuclear proliferation, the lives of Christians must be the "light of the world." We must be, as Jesus called us, a city on a hill that cannot be hidden.

I was in Nepal, in the shadow of the Himalayas, when Jerry Falwell was buried.

In an Internet café in Kathmandu, I pulled up the news on a very slow computer. A student had been arrested at the funeral, I read, with explosives in his car. I recognized the name and the face. He was one of my students. Definitely *not* a young champion for Christ, I thought.

I had just seen Dr. Falwell a few days earlier at a department function, a good-bye ceremony for two long-standing faculty members. He was typically gracious in his comments and more nostalgic than usual when he reflected on the early years of his ministry. I noticed at the time how colorless he looked, how slowly he was moving. He didn't seem well, so I was not really surprised when the e-mail popped up on my computer the next Tuesday morning: "Faculty and staff are requested to gather in the sanctuary of Thomas Road Baptist Church at 2:00 p.m. for an announcement about Dr. Falwell."

The graduation ceremonies—only five days later—were bittersweet. Newt Gingrich delivered the commencement address, and two thousand graduates received their diplomas, including my wife, Janel, who graduated with a master's degree.

The next day I flew to Nepal on a mission trip with my pastor. I found myself in the small border town of Kakarbhitta, where the edges of four countries—Nepal, India, Bangladesh, and Bhutan—nearly merged. The first night we were there, Troy and I walked up to the border, which was just a hundred yards away from the Hotel Rajat. We stopped along the street in front of a *mandir*, a small Hindu temple, where worshipers were singing and a man was dancing before a statue of Krishna. I was suddenly taken back to my childhood in Africa. There I learned that the gospel has power to transform lives bound by idolatry, be it the idolatry of stones and sticks, of Hindu gods and goddesses, or even of American materialism and self-reliance.

What answers that idolatry? What answers the longing of the human heart, wherever that heart beats? What brings hope into a dark world?

I stood there on the street, dazed from jet lag and the whirlwind of events, listening to the hypnotic music. The light flickered from the mandir. The rickshaws glided by. My mind went back to the graduation ceremony that had so unexpectedly become part celebration and part memorial service. Driving home, Janel had showed me the small packet of materials given that day to each graduate. "They gave us this pin too," she said. I recognized it instantly. "Keep that," I said. "It's a classic."

Janel handed the little pin to me, and I closed it in my fist. It was the trademark of Falwell's years on television—a lapel pin that predated the Moral Majority and reduced everything that really matters to two simple words: *Jesus First.*

ACKNOWLEDGMENTS

[to come from author]

215

ABOUT THE AUTHOR

*T*o come

NOTES

INTRODUCTION

Burton Mack declared. As quoted in Charlotte Allen, "The Search for a No-Frills Jesus," The Atlantic Monthly (December 1996).

Romanitas. Tertullian used the term in De Pallio. The term Romanitas is complex, as Tertullian was really defending the legitimacy of North African culture (not specifically "Christian" values). Still, the consciousness of Christianity as a culture brought about this awareness of Roman culture that Tertullian was denouncing.

CHAPTER ONE: THE BATTLE IS ENGAGED

Epigraph. Cal Thomas and Ed Dobson. Blinded by Might (Grand Rapids, MI: Zondervan, 1999).

Richard Viguerie had predicted. In an interview in 1976, as quoted in Herbert F. Vetter, ed., Speak Out against the New Right (Boston: PUBLISHER, 1982).

According to Weyrich. See Dan Gilgoff, The Jesus Machine (New York: St. Martin's Press, 2007), 78–79.

President Nixon. Source for IRS policy statement: www.presidency.ucsb.edu.

Billy Graham described this. As quoted in James Reichley, Religion in American Public Life (Washington, DC: Brookings Institution Press, 1985), 147.

Senator Sam Ervin. As quoted in Stephen J. Whitfield, "Separation Anxiety: From Founders to Fundamentalists— Separation between Church and State," Judaism (spring 1995).

George Andrews, a congressman. Ibid.

A columnist for the Globe and Mail. TO COME FROM AUTHOR.

Time described Falwell. "The Rev. Jerry Falwell Says God Has a Message for Caesar," Time (October 1, 1979).

Two eminent social historians. Quotations from Lipset and Raab in this passage are taken from "The Election and the Evangelicals," retrieved online at www.harvardsquarelibrary.org.

In Weyrich's alternate time line. See Gilgoff, The Jesus Machine, 85.

The lead in the New York Times article. Wayne King, "Pat Robertson: A Candidate of Contradictions," New York Times (February 27, 1988).

Reed boldly told the Los Angeles Times. As quoted May 1, 1990, by the Religious News Service.

"I paint my face and travel at night." Virginia Norfolk-Pilot (November 9, 1991).

"Now comes the revolution." Richard Viguerie, as quoted in David D. Kirkpatrick, "Some Bush Supports Say They Anticipate a 'Revolution,'" New York Times (November 4, 2004).

Rod Dreher. As quoted by ABC News (May 4, 2007), retrieved on www.abcnews.go.com.

The morning after Reed's primary defeat. Shaila Dewan, "Ralph Reed Loses Georgia Primary Race," New York Times (July 19, 2006).

Reed wrote to Abramoff in an e-mail. As quoted in Susan Schmidt and James V. Grimaldi, "Panel Says Abramoff Laundered Tribal Funds," Washington Post (June 23, 2005).

One historian has written. Bryan F. Le Beau, "The Political Mobilization of the New Christian Right," retrieved from http://are.as.wvu.edu/lebeau3.htm.

CHAPTER TWO: HOW CHRISTIAN A NATION?

Epigraph. John MacArthur, "The Christian and Government: The Christian Responsibility to Government, Part 1." Transcription of sermon retrieved from www.biblebb.com.

Alexis de Tocqueville's. The phrase "America is great because America is good" has been demonstrated to be a spurious quotation; it was not included in Tocqueville's Democracy in America. This hasn't stopped politicians (including Presidents Eisenhower and Reagan) and evangelical leaders from "quoting" these words as authoritative. For details on this legendary quote, see John J. Pitney Jr., "The Tocqueville Fraud," Weekly Standard (November 13, 1995).

Gettysburg. Official text and draft copies are quoted from the Library of Congress Web site: www.loc.gov.

But Lincoln repeatedly confessed his fatalism. Lincoln quotations are taken from Allen C. Guelzo, "Abraham Lincoln and the Doctrine of Necessity," Journal of the Abraham Lincoln Association, vol. 18, no. 1 (winter 1997).

John Adams and John Hancock. The story of Adams and Hancock at the home of Reverend Jonas Clarke in Lexington, Massachusetts, on the eve of the Revolutionary War (April 18, 1775) has been recounted many times. Their statement was reportedly a response to British Major Pitcairn's demand for them to surrender. See, for example, the Web site of the Lexington Historical Society: www.lexingtonhistory.org.

Thomas Jefferson. The statement "I am a real Christian" is found in his letter to Charles Thomson (January 9, 1816).

In a pamphlet entitled. Pamphlet by James Dobson, as quoted in Albert Soto, "The American Rebellion," retrieved from: www.atruechurch.info/revolution.html.

A man who wrote to the Danbury Baptists. Jefferson's letter (which contains the famous words "a wall of separation between Church and State") is found at the Library of Congress Web site: www.loc.gov.

A retired president of Yale University. Theodore Woolsey, History, Essays, Orations, and Other Documents of the Sixth General Conference of the Evangelical Alliance, held in New York, October 2–12, 1873, edited by Philip Schaff and S. Irenaeus Prime (New York: PUBLISHER, 1874).

Woolsey contended that. Ira Mark Ellman, "The Misguided Movement to Revive Fault Divorce," published in Martin King Whyte, ed., Marriage in America (Lanham, MD: Rowman & Littlefield Publishers, Inc., 2000), 189.

The substance of our national Promise. Herbert Croly's The Promise of American Life (1909) is in the public domain and is available online at www.gutenberg.org.

Scripture is clear that Israel was the only nation. We see Israel's role (to be a witness of God's glory, to reveal God's holiness, to deliver God's law, and to usher the Messiah into the world) described in Isaiah 43:1-7; Leviticus 19:2; and Isaiah 42:1-7, among other passages.

Romans saw the blessing of Jupiter. One of the recurring themes of the great Roman epic Virgil's Aeneid (written ca. 27 BC) is that Rome was a chosen people, living out its destiny under the guidance of the Roman gods.

CHAPTER THREE: RETHINKING THE SHINING CITY

Epigraph. Gary Bauer quoted from his campaign literature archived on www.4president.org. Kevin Phillips quoted from American Theocracy (New York: Viking, 2006), 129.

Winthrop preached a sermon. "A Model of Christian Charity" can be found online at www.winthropsociety.org.

Samuel Langdon. Quotations from Langdon and Jefferson are taken from "Manifest Destiny: America the New Israel," retrieved from http://gbgm-umc.org. Emphasis is mine.

We Americans are the peculiar, chosen people. Quotations from Melville here, and on subsequent pages, are found in his novel White Jacket (1850), which is available online at www.gutenberg.org. Emphasis is mine.

The letters Columbus sent home. Columbus is quoted from his "Letter to King Ferdinand of Spain, describing the results of the first voyage" (1493). Translated text is available online at http://xroads.virginia.edu. "We can convert these gentle people" is a loose paraphrase taken from this sentence: "I gave them a thousand handsome good things, which I had brought, in order that they might conceive affection for us, and, more than that, might become Christians and be inclined to the love and service of Your Highnesses." Emphasis is mine.

Arthur Barlow. Barlow and Thomas Hariot are quoted in documents retrieved from http://xroads.virginia.edu.

A cartoon in the New Yorker. Donald Reilly's cartoon appeared in the June 4, 1974, edition.

In my mind it was a tall, proud city. The text of Reagan's farewell address is found at www.reaganfoundation.org.

Winthrop's conception of social structure. The text of "A Model of Christian Charity" is found at www.winthropsociety.org.

Emil Reich. Quoted by Herbert Croly in the first paragraph of The Promise of American Life (New York: PUBLISHER, 1909).

Teddy Roosevelt described. The text of The Winning of the West is available online at www.gutenberg.org.

The seductiveness of self-reliance. Joel Osteen's Your Best Life Now has been popular enough to spin off related devotionals and even a board game.

Gene Veith. As quoted in James Montgomery Boice, "The New Pragmatism," available online at www.the-highway.com.

CHAPTER FOUR: THE LONG DEFEAT

Epigraph. Jerry Falwell is quoted from his July 6, 1997, sermon, "Rebuilding America's Walls," available online at www.trbc.com.

Studies have shown that close to 90 percent. "Scientists and Religion in America," Scientific American (September 1999).

Voltaire. From his letter to Frederick the Great (1767).

Mark Twain. TO COME FROM AUTHOR.

H. L. Mencken. Quotation from H. L. Mencken's Notebooks (New York: Alfred A. Knopf, 1956).

Science can help us to get over this craven fear. "Why I Am Not a Christian" was delivered as a lecture and published in 1927.

The book was reviewed. Quotations are from Peter Hitchens, "Hitchens vs. Hitchens," Daily Mail (June 2, 2007).

How do religious Americans compare. Arthur C. Brooks, "The Ennui of Saint Teresa," The Wall Street Journal (September 30, 2007).

Curiously, the West hardly factors. Wallbuilders, founded by Christian historian David Barton as an educational institution that sponsors lectures and publications, is one notable example of this evangelical emphasis on the Eastern seaboard and, specifically, colonial American history.

On his feet were deerskin moccasins. Quotation from Cooper, The Pioneers, available online at www.gutenberg.org.

In the words of Lewis. R. W. B. Lewis, The American Adam (CITY: PUBLISHER, 1955), 91.

As another scholar put it. David Noble, "Cooper, Leatherstocking and the Death of the American Adam," American Quarterly, vol. 16, no. 3 (autumn 1963): 420.

Then God took man. Translation of Pico della Mirandola from Ernst Cassirer, Paul Oskar Kristeller, and John H. Randall, eds., The Renaissance Philosophy of Man (CITY: PUBLISHER, 1948). Emphasis is mine.

One reviewer in the New York Times. Leon Wieseltier, New York Times (February 19, 2006).

The new world created the modern era. Wallace Stegner summarizes Walter Webb's thesis in Marking the Sparrow's Fall: The Making of the American West (New York: Henry Holt and Company, 1998), 191–192.

The original Puritans. Lewis Perry, Intellectual Life in America: A History (CITY: PUBLISHER, 1984), 45.

Historian Kenneth Lockridge. The term "Christian Utopian Closed Corporate Communities" is introduced in New England Town: The First Hundred Years (CITY: PUBLISHER, 1970), 16.

Speaking of both Americas. Quotations from Llosa and Fuentes are found in Dinesh D'Souza, "The Crimes of Christopher Columbus," First Things 57 (November 1995): 25–33.

Niebuhr pleaded instead. Quotation is from Cushing Strout, who is summarizing Niebuhr's perspective in "Niebuhr's Irony and American History," American Quarterly, vol. 5, no. 2 (summer 1953): 175.

The first sentence of Paul Johnson's. A History of the American People (New York: HarperCollins, 1998).

Scripture always assumes a distance. The importance of the idea of separation from the ungodly world system around us is underscored by especially strong language: "Ye adulterers and adulteresses, know ye not that the friendship of the world is enmity with God? Whosoever therefore will be a friend of the world is the enemy of God" (James 4:4, kjv). See also 2 Corinthians 6:17.

Toward the end of his life. Falwell is quoted in Lev Chavets, "A Holy Warrior, Holy Committed," Los Angeles Times (May 16, 2007).

CHAPTER FIVE: BACK TO THE BEGINNING

Epigraph. John R. W. Stott, Basic Christianity (CITY: PUBLISHER, 1958), 11.

Concerning the Oklahoma City bombing. Quotations from columnist Ann Coulter are documented in an Associated Press article by Philip Elliott published in the Washington Post (June 9, 2006).

John MacArthur has argued. Quotations from Why Government Can't Save You (Nashville: Thomas Nelson, 2000), 6.

But all this documentary evidence. The textual evidence is laid out impressively at the Wallbuilders Web site: www.wallbuilders.com.

Many of the "heroes of the faith." David Barton, "Was the American Revolution a Biblically Justified Act?" retrieved from www.wallbuilders.com.

Thus, upon a careful review of the apostle's reasoning. Jonathan Mayhew's sermon "A Discourse Concerning Unlimited Submission and Non-Resistance to the Higher Powers" is widely available online (see, for example, www.lawandliberty.org). A standard text is Perry Miller and Thomas H. Johnson, The Puritans: A Sourcebook of Their Writings (New York: Dover Publications, 2001). Emphasis is mine.

The religious tolerance that was the normal Greek and Roman practice. E. R. Dodds, Pagan and Christian in an Age of Anxiety (CITY: PUBLISHER, 1991), 131.

Christianity was open to all. Ibid., 134.

In a time when earthly life was increasingly devalued. Ibid., 136.

Their promptitude in bringing material help. Ibid, 138.

Harvey Mansfield. "Atheist Tracts: God, They're Predictable," The Weekly Standard, vol. 12, no. 45 (August 13, 2007).

As Bickerton put it. William H. Calvin and Derek Bickerton, Lingua ex Machina: Reconciling Darwin and Chomsky with the Human Brain (CITY: PUBLISHER, 2000), 104.

Chomsky's skepticism has earned him the scorn. Steven Pinker discusses the term "crypto-creationist" in The Language Instinct (CITY: PUBLISHER, 1994), 355.

A key plank in Emerson's argument. Emerson is quoted from "The American Scholar," available online at www.gutenberg.org.

As one scholar has described it. Harold Fromm, "Overcoming the Oversoul: Emerson's Evolutionary Existentialism," The Hudson Review (spring 2004).

CHAPTER SIX: WHAT'S WORTH FIGHTING FOR?

Epigraph. R. Albert Mohler, Jr., "The Origins of Life: An Evangelical Baptist View," retrieved from www.npr.org.

90 percent are opting for abortion. This according to Amy Harmon, "Prenatal Test Puts Down Syndrome in Hard Focus," New York Times (May 9, 2007).

That practice in ancient Greece and Rome. TO COME FROM AUTHOR.

Carl Sagan's popular Cosmos. First aired in 1980 as a documentary series on PBS, Cosmos came out in book form in 1985.

In one of his many works of Darwinian apologetics. Richard Dawkins, River out of Eden (CITY: PUBLISHER, 1995), 18.

Consider the case of Jennifer Raper. As reported by the Associated Press (March 7, 2007); article retrieved from www.boston.com.

Life is the great issue the church cut its public policy teeth on. See the extensive historical survey by Alvin J. Schmidt, Under the Influence: How Christianity Transformed Civilization (Grand Rapids, MI: Zondervan, 2001), 48–78.

As R. Albert Mohler Jr. puts it. "The Origins of Life: An Evangelical Baptist View," retrieved from www.npr.org.

In 374 Basil's efforts helped to persuade. Schmidt, Under the Influence, 59.

Didache. Quotation from the translation by Kirsopp Lake in the Loeb Classical Library, available online at www.earlychristianwritings.com.

By the ruling of the Supreme Court. Francis Schaeffer, How Should We Then Live? (CITY: PUBLISHER, 1976), 223.

I believe the majority of the silent majority. Ibid., 227.

The evolution of Schaeffer's thought. Quotation from The Complete Works of Francis A. Schaeffer (Wheaton, IL: Crossway Books, 1985), 346.

Every life means every life, without exception. Quotations in this passage from David Gushee are found in "Retrieving a Consistent Pro-Life Ethic," retrieved from www.abpnews.com.

Senator Hillary Clinton. As reported by Patrick D. Healy, "Clinton Seeking Shared Ground over Abortions," New York Times (January 25, 2005).

The Reed letter. As quoted in Thomas B. Edsall, "Another Stumble for Ralph Reed's Beleaguered Campaign," Washington Post (May 29, 2006).

Already in 1976. How is this trend line apparent in America today? The controversy over the removal of Terry Schiavo's feeding tube in 2005 is one example. The controversy—in 2001 and following—over public funding of embryonic stem cell research is another. The very definition of life is foundational to these public policy disputes.

Peter Singer. When asked directly by the editorial staff of Independent, a leading British newspaper, "Would you kill a disabled baby?" Singer replied, "Yes, if that was in the best interests of the baby and of the family as a whole." Independent (September 11, 2006).

MIT research Steven Pinker. Pinker's Darwinian interpretation of infanticide is related in his article "Why They Kill Their Newborns," New York Times (November 2, 1997).

"Suicide clinics." The case of the sixty-seven-year-old German woman was reported by Bojan Pancevski, "Swiss Suicide Clinics Helping Depressives Die," Telegraph (March 6, 2007).

One Oakland-based nonprofit group. Quotation is taken from Exhale's Web site: www.4exhale.org/values.php.

CHAPTER SEVEN: A SIMPLE CALL TO VIRTUE

Epigraph. John R. W. Stott, The Message of the Sermon on the Mount (Downers Grove, IL: InterVarsity Press, 1978), 15.

These issues of development and change in the Scriptures. M. James Sawyer, "Dispensationalism," in The Blackwell Encyclopedia of Modern Christian Thought, edited by Alister McGrath (Malden, MA: Blackwell Publishing Inc., 1993).

Ryrie argued. Charles Ryrie, Dispensationalism Today (Chicago: Moody, 1965), 109.

A good deal in the sermon on the mount. Arno Gaebelein, The Gospel of Matthew (Neptune, NJ: Loizeaux Brothers, 1961), 109.

Karlgaard writes. Quotations are taken from Rich Karlgaard, "The American Dream and the Gospel of Success," retrieved from www.forbes.com/digitalrules/2007/10/the-american-dr.html.

Cardinal Ratzinger. Quotation from Cardinal Ratzinger's homily at the opening of the papal conclave that would elect him pope, delivered April 18, 2005. Text available online at www.ncronline.org. Emphasis is mine.

This struggle of the heart. Gaebelein, The Gospel of Matthew, 109.